Home-Tested Casserole Recipes

Publications International, Ltd.

Favorite Brand Name Recipes at www.fbnr.com

Photography on pages 9, 13, 17, 25, 33, 35, 45, 57, 61, 63, 65, 69, 87, 93, 95, 113, 115, 117, 119, 123, 125, 129, 133, 143, 145, 147, 149, 151, 157, 161, 171, 173, 177, 185, 193, 197, 201, 205, 209 and 211 by Proffitt Photography, Ltd., Chicago
Photographer: Laurie Proffitt
Photographer's Assistant: Chad Evans
Food Stylist: Carol Smoler
Assistant Food Stylists: Liza Brown, Alison Reich
Prop Stylist: Paula Walters

Pictured on the front cover: Zucornchile Rajas Bake *(page 88),* submitted by Elaine Sweet (inset photo).

Pictured on the back cover *(from top to bottom):* Cha-Cha-Cha Casserole *(page 94)* and Baked Risotto with Asparagus, Spinach and Parmesan *(page 132).*

ISBN: 0-7853-8046-9

Library of Congress Control Number: 2003105300

Manufactured in China.

8 7 6 5 4 3 2 1

Microwave Cooking: Microwave ovens vary in wattage. Use the cooking times as guidelines and check for doneness before adding more time.

TABLE OF CONTENTS

Many of the recipes in this book were submitted by home cooks as part of a contest previously sponsored by this publisher. Don't miss the prize-winning recipes on pages 18, 88, 98, 102, 194 and 202.

COME HOME
TO CASSEROLES

From a spicy tamale pie with a Texas accent to a Minnesota hot dish of beef and egg noodles, every family and every region of the country has its favorite casseroles. It's not surprising that casseroles are such an important part of home cooking. They're an economical way to stretch a pound or two of meat to feed a crowd and an easy way to serve a well-balanced meal in a single dish. Versatile casseroles can use up leftovers, grace an elegant buffet table, or travel beautifully to a potluck or a church supper.

The recipes in Home-Tested Casseroles are from kitchens like yours. This is cooking that's smart enough to utilize up-to-date ingredients like polenta, salsa and risotto without ever getting faddish or contrived. Because these recipes come from folks who know how to get dinner on the table with a minimum of fuss, you'll find practical shortcuts, not tricky techniques. Best of all, you'll discover dozens of ways to fill your dinner hour with the warmth and comfort of home cooking at its very best. As anyone who loves casseroles knows, no fancy restaurant meal can ever come close.

PANTRY
PROVISIONS

Here's a basic list of pantry staples that should be part of every casserole cook's kitchen. As with casseroles themselves, it should be adjusted to suit you and your family's individual tastes.

Grains and Pasta
pasta, (long spaghetti types, shorter macaroni types, egg noodles and lasagna noodles)
polenta (quick cooking or ready-to-serve)
rice (white, brown and/or wild, flavored rice mixes, arborio rice for risotto)

Canned Goods
beans (black, kidney, chick-peas, white, etc)
broth and bouillon
chicken, ham or corned beef
condensed soup
crabmeat
corn, creamed and regular
olives
pimientos
spaghetti sauce
tomato sauce and paste
tomatoes (whole and diced with herbs, spices and chilies)
tuna
vegetables

Condiments
hot sauce
ketchup and barbecue sauce
mayonnaise
mustard
olive and vegetable oil
sour cream or yogurt
soy sauce
salsa
vinegar (white, balsamic, wine and cider)
Worcestershire sauce

Dry Goods
biscuit mix
bread crumbs
cereal
flour
nuts
stuffing mix

Vegetables and Fruit
frozen vegetables
garlic
lemons and limes
onions
potatoes (fresh and frozen)

CASSEROLE
VOLUMES

Since casseroles come in many sizes and shapes, choosing the right one for a recipe can be confusing. Wherever possible, a size or volume has been suggested for each recipe. To measure the volume of any casserole, simply fill it with measured quarts of water to determine how many it holds. If you don't have the recommended casserole, substitute any ovenproof baking dish in a size that is as large or slightly larger than the recommended one. (*A larger dish may require a shorter baking time, so check sooner than recommended in the recipe.*)

If you don't have a:	Use a:
1-quart casserole	8×6-inch baking dish
1-1/2-quart casserole	8×8-inch baking dish
2-quart casserole	8×8-inch or 11×7-inch baking dish
2-1/2-quart casserole	9×9-inch baking dish
3- to 4-quart casserole	13×9-inch baking dish or Dutch oven
5 quart casserole	large Dutch oven or roasting pan

CHOOSING A CASSEROLE DISH

Whether you're planning to purchase a new casserole dish or just deciding which of your current ones will work for a particular recipe, it helps to know the pros and cons of the many different casserole materials.

Casserole Dishes	Advantages	Disadvantages
enameled cast iron	retains heat well, durable, suitable for range-top use	heavy, usually costly, can chip
stainless steel	durable, inexpensive, suitable for range-top use	poor heat conductor unless bottom is lined with copper or aluminum
oven-proof porcelain or ceramic	inexpensive, retains heat fairly well	cannot be used on range-top, may crack or chip
oven-proof glass	inexpensive, retains heat fairly well	cannot be used on range-top
cast iron	excellent long-term heat retention, very inexpensive, suitable for range-top use	reacts with acidic ingredients, very heavy
aluminum	heats quickly and also cools down quickly, very inexpensive, lightweight	reacts with acidic ingredients, stains easily and can warp, not dishwasher safe
hard-adonized aluminum	retains heat well, suitable for range-top use	expensive, not dishwasher safe

GREAT
GROUND MEAT

Pizza Casserole
Richard White | Lewistown, Pennsylvania

2 cups uncooked rotini or other short pasta
1½ to 2 pounds ground beef
1 medium onion, chopped
  Salt and pepper
1 can (about 15 ounces) pizza sauce
1 can (8 ounces) tomato sauce
1 can (6 ounces) tomato paste
½ teaspoon sugar
½ teaspoon garlic salt
½ teaspoon dried oregano leaves
2 cups (8 ounces) shredded mozzarella cheese
12 to 15 slices pepperoni

1. Preheat oven to 350°F. Cook rotini according to package directions. Set aside.

2. Meanwhile, cook and stir ground beef and onion in large skillet over medium-high heat until meat is no longer pink. Season with salt and pepper. Set aside.

3. Combine rotini, pizza sauce, tomato sauce, tomato paste, sugar, garlic salt and oregano in large bowl. Add beef mixture and combine.

4. Place half of mixture in 3-quart casserole and top with 1 cup cheese. Repeat layers. Arrange pepperoni slices on top. Bake 25 to 30 minutes or until heated through and cheese is melted.

Makes 6 servings

Zesty Turkey Pot Pie

1 tablespoon vegetable oil
1 small onion, finely chopped
1 jalapeño pepper,* cored, seeded and minced
1 pound ground turkey
1 package (16 ounces) frozen mixed vegetables
½ teaspoon dried thyme leaves
½ teaspoon black pepper
2 cans (10¾ ounces each) condensed golden mushroom soup, undiluted
1 package (11 ounces) refrigerated breadsticks (12 breadsticks)

Jalapeño peppers can sting and irritate the skin; wear rubber gloves when handling peppers and do not touch eyes. Wash hands after handling peppers.

1. Preheat oven to 350°F. Grease 13×9-inch casserole.

2. Heat oil in large skillet over medium heat. Add onion and jalapeño pepper; cook and stir 5 minutes or until tender. Crumble turkey into skillet; cook until no longer pink, stirring to separate.

3. Stir in vegetables, thyme and pepper. Cook 5 minutes until vegetables are thawed. Stir in soup. Cook 5 to 10 minutes or until mixture is heated through. Spoon turkey mixture into prepared casserole.

4. Pull and stretch breadsticks to lengthen, pressing ends together if necessary to reach across baking dish. Arrange breadsticks in lattice pattern over turkey, trimming ends. Bake 15 to 20 minutes or until breadsticks are golden brown. *Makes 6 servings*

Note: Mixture must be hot when spooned into casserole or breadsticks will be gummy on the bottom.

Zesty Turkey Pot Pie

Meat Crust Pie

Chris Gelinskey | Oconomowoc, Wisconsin

  1 pound ground beef
  2 cans (8 ounces each) tomato sauce, divided
  ½ cup seasoned dry bread crumbs
  ½ cup chopped green bell pepper, divided
  ¼ cup minced onion
  1 teaspoon salt, divided
  ⅛ teaspoon dried oregano leaves
  ⅛ teaspoon pepper
  1 cup water
1⅓ cups instant rice
  1 cup grated Cheddar cheese, divided

1. Preheat oven to 350°F. Combine beef, ½ cup tomato sauce, bread crumbs, ¼ cup bell pepper, onion, ½ teaspoon salt, oregano and pepper in large bowl; mix well. Pat onto bottom and side of ungreased 9-inch, deep-dish pie plate.

2. Bring water and remaining ½ teaspoon salt to boil in medium saucepan. Stir in rice; cover and remove from heat. Let stand 5 minutes or until water is absorbed. Add remaining 1½ cups tomato sauce, ½ cup cheese and remaining ¼ cup bell pepper to rice and combine. Spoon rice mixture into meat shell. Cover with foil and bake 25 minutes.

3. Remove from oven and drain fat carefully, holding a pan lid in place to keep pie from sliding. Top with remaining ½ cup cheese and return to oven. Bake uncovered 10 to 15 minutes or until cheese melts. Carefully drain fat again. Cut into wedges to serve.

Makes 6 to 8 servings

Meat Crust Pie

Indian-Style Lamb & Chick-Peas

Marilyn Pocius | Oak Park, Illinois

2 tablespoons butter, divided
1 onion, chopped
3 cloves garlic, chopped
2 teaspoons finely chopped fresh ginger
1 pound ground lamb
2 tablespoons lemon juice
   Salt and pepper
1 pound (about 3 medium) fresh tomatoes, diced
1 tablespoon curry powder
½ teaspoon ground red pepper
⅛ teaspoon cinnamon
⅛ teaspoon nutmeg
2 cans (about 14 ounces each) chick-peas, drained and rinsed
¾ cup plain yogurt (not non-fat)
½ cup dry bread crumbs

1. Preheat oven to 350°F. Melt 1 tablespoon butter in large skillet. Cook and stir onion, garlic and ginger over medium-high heat for 2 minutes or until they begin to soften. Add lamb; cook, stirring to break up meat, until it is no longer pink. Season with salt and pepper.

2. Add tomatoes, curry powder, red pepper, cinnamon and nutmeg; cook and stir about five minutes until well combined. Remove from heat. Add chick-peas and yogurt; stir to combine.

3. Transfer mixture to 2- to 2½ quart casserole. Sprinkle bread crumbs on top and dot with remaining 1 tablespoon butter. Bake 30 minutes or until bubbly and lightly browned.

Makes 6 to 8 servings

Oven-Baked Black Bean Chili

Carolyn Blakemore | Fairmont, West Virginia

1½ pounds lean ground beef
¼ cup chopped sweet onion
¼ cup chopped green bell pepper
1 can (about 15 ounces) black beans, rinsed and drained
1 can (14½ ounces) diced tomatoes with green chilies
1 can (about 14 ounces) beef broth
1 can (8 ounces) tomato sauce
5 tablespoons chili powder
1 tablespoon sugar
1 tablespoon ground cumin
1 teaspoon dried minced onion
⅛ teaspoon garlic powder
⅛ teaspoon ground ginger
2 cups (8 ounces) shredded Mexican cheese blend

1. Preheat oven to 350°F. Cook and stir beef, onion and bell pepper in large skillet over medium-high heat until meat is no longer pink. Drain and transfer to 4-quart casserole.

2. Add remaining ingredients, except cheese, and stir to combine. Cover and bake 30 minutes, stirring every 10 minutes or so. Uncover, top with cheese, and return to oven about 5 minutes or until cheese melts.   *Makes 6 to 8 servings*

Carolyn says: This chili is great served with Mexican-style cornbread!

Pastitsio

8 ounces uncooked ziti or elbow macaroni
1 pound ground lamb or beef
½ cup chopped onion
1 clove garlic, chopped fine
1 can (about 8 ounces) tomato sauce
½ teaspoon dried oregano leaves
½ teaspoon black pepper
¼ teaspoon ground cinnamon
1 cup grated Parmesan cheese, divided
2 tablespoons butter
2 tablespoons all-purpose flour
1½ cups milk
1 egg, beaten

1. Preheat oven to 350°F. Spray 9-inch baking dish with nonstick cooking spray.

2. Cook pasta according to package directions. Drain and reserve.

3. Cook and stir lamb, onion and garlic in large skillet over medium-high heat until lamb is no longer pink; drain fat. Stir in tomato sauce, oregano, pepper and cinnamon. Reduce heat to low and simmer 10 minutes.

4. Layer ½ of pasta in prepared baking dish. Top with meat mixture, then remaining pasta.

5. For sauce, melt butter in medium saucepan. Stir in flour. Cook and stir 1 minute. Whisk in milk. Cook, stirring constantly until thickened, about 6 minutes. Place beaten egg in small bowl; stir some of sauce into egg. Return egg mixture to saucepan; cook and stir 2 minutes. Stir in ¾ cup Parmesan.

6. Pour sauce mixture over pasta layer. Sprinkle with remaining ¼ cup Parmesan. Bake 30 to 40 minutes until heated through and golden brown. *Makes 6 servings*

Athens Casserole

Barbara J. Dickinson | Harbor City, New Jersey

    2 tablespoons vegetable oil
1½ pounds eggplant, peeled, cut crosswise into ¼-inch slices
1½ pounds ground beef
    2 cups chopped onion
    1 medium green bell pepper, cut into strips
    1 medium yellow bell pepper, cut into strips
    1 medium red bell pepper, cut into strips
    ¼ cup chopped fresh parsley
    ¼ cup red wine
    1 teaspoon garlic powder
    1 teaspoon ground cinnamon
       Salt and pepper
    2 cans (28 ounces each) stewed tomatoes
    8 ounces feta cheese, crumbled
    4 eggs, beaten
    ½ cup bread crumbs

1. Preheat oven to 350°F.

2. Heat oil in large skillet over medium-high heat. Add eggplant and brown on both sides, 5 to 7 minutes; set aside on paper towels to drain.

3. In same skillet, cook and stir ground beef, onions and bell peppers over medium heat until onion is transparent and beef is browned. Add parsley, wine, garlic powder and cinnamon; mix well. Season with salt and pepper.

4. Pour ⅓ of tomatoes into 13×9-inch baking dish. Add ⅓ of eggplant, ⅓ of beef mixture and ⅓ of cheese. Repeat layers until all ingredients are used. Pour eggs on top and sprinkle with bread crumbs.

5. Bake 45 minutes or until heated through and bubbly.

Makes 10 servings

Athens Casserole   19

Chanci's Goulash

Chanci McKinnon | Rosenberg, Texas

1 tablespoon margarine
2 pounds ground beef
1 package (8 ounces) shell macaroni, cooked
3 onions, chopped
1 green bell pepper, chopped
1 can (15 ounces) whole kernel corn
1 cup sherry
1 can (6 ounces) tomato paste
1 cup (4 ounces) shredded sharp Cheddar cheese
1 can (4 ounces) sliced mushrooms, drained
3 cloves garlic, minced
1 tablespoon brown sugar
1 tablespoon Worcestershire sauce
1 tablespoon chili powder
2 teaspoons salt
¼ teaspoon pepper

1. Melt margarine in large skillet over medium-high heat. Cook and stir beef until no longer pink. Drain fat.

2. Place meat in large bowl and add all remaining ingredients. Stir to combine. Pour into two 1½-quart casseroles.

3. Refrigerate overnight to blend flavors. Bake, covered, in preheated 350°F oven 1 hour or until heated through. *Makes 8 to 10 servings*

Home Cook's HINT

When pasta will be added to a casserole and cooked longer with other ingredients, it's very important not to overcook it in the first place. Don't necessarily trust the cooking times printed on the package. The best test is to remove a piece and taste it. It should still be a bit firm.

Zucchini Parmigiana Casserole

Tanya Bates | Clearwater, Florida

½ cup flour
3 eggs, beaten
2 cups Italian-seasoned bread crumbs
6 cups sliced zucchini
½ cup olive oil
1 pound lean ground beef
½ pound ground sausage
1 cup chopped onion
1 tablespoon minced garlic
¼ cup chopped fresh basil
2 tablespoons chopped fresh oregano
4 cups tomato sauce
2 cups (8 ounces) shredded mozzarella
¼ cup grated Parmesan cheese
4 tablespoons chopped fresh parsley

1. Preheat oven to 350°F. Place flour, eggs and bread crumbs in separate shallow bowls. Dip zucchini in flour, egg, then bread crumbs to coat. Heat olive oil in medium skillet over medium-high heat. Brown zucchini on both sides in batches; season with salt and pepper. Drain zucchini on paper towels. Drain fat from skillet.

2. Add ground beef, sausage, onion and garlic to skillet. Cook and stir until meat is no longer pink. Drain fat. Stir in basil and oregano.

3. Layer ½ of tomato sauce, ½ of zucchini, ½ of meat mixture, ½ of mozzarella and ½ of Parmesan in 4-quart casserole. Repeat layers.

4. Bake 30 minutes or until heated through and cheese is melted. Top with parsley. *Makes 6 servings*

Old-Fashioned Cabbage Rolls

Arnita Jones | McKenzie, Tennessee

½ pound *each* ground beef, ground veal and ground pork
1 small onion, chopped
2 eggs, lightly beaten
½ cup dry bread crumbs
1 teaspoon salt
1 teaspoon molasses
¼ teaspoon ground ginger
¼ teaspoon ground nutmeg
¼ teaspoon ground allspice
1 large head cabbage, separated into leaves
3 cups boiling water
¼ cup (½ stick) butter or margarine
½ cup milk, or more as needed
1 tablespoon cornstarch

1. Combine meats and onion in large bowl. Combine eggs, bread crumbs, salt, molasses, ginger, nutmeg and allspice in medium bowl; mix well. Add to meat mixture and combine well.

2. Drop cabbage leaves into boiling water for 3 minutes. Remove with slotted spoon, reserving ½ cup of boiling liquid.

3. Preheat oven to 375°F. Place about 2 tablespoons of meat mixture about 1 inch from stem end of each leaf. Fold sides in and roll up, fastening with toothpicks, if necessary.

4. Heat butter in large skillet over medium-high heat. Add cabbage rolls (3 or 4 at a time) to skillet and brown on all sides. Arrange rolls, seam-side down in a single layer in casserole. Combine reserved liquid with butter remaining in skillet and pour over cabbage rolls.

5. Bake 1 hour. Remove and carefully drain accumulated pan juices into measuring cup. Add enough milk to pan juices to equal one cup.

6. Pour milk mixture into small saucepan, stir in cornstarch and bring to a boil, stirring constantly until sauce is thickened. Pour over cabbage rolls and bake 15 minutes more or until sauce is browned and cabbage is very tender. *Makes 8 servings*

Spicy Beefy Noodles
Marlene Roberts | Moore, Oklahoma

1½ pounds ground beef
1 small onion, minced
1 clove garlic, minced
1 tablespoon chili powder
1 teaspoon paprika
⅛ teaspoon *each* dried basil, dill weed, thyme and marjoram
   Salt and pepper
1 can (10 ounces) diced tomatoes with green chilies, undrained
1 can (8 ounces) tomato sauce
1 cup water
3 tablespoons Worcestershire sauce
1 package (about 10 ounces) egg noodles, cooked according to
   package directions
½ cup *each* shredded Cheddar, mozzarella, Pepper-Jack and
   provolone cheeses

1. Cook and stir ground beef with onion and garlic in large skillet over medium heat until meat is no longer pink; drain well. Add chili powder, paprika, basil, dill, thyme and marjoram. Season with salt and pepper. Cook and stir 2 minutes.

2. Add diced tomatoes, tomato sauce, water and Worcestershire sauce. Mix well and simmer, covered, 20 minutes.

2. In microwave-safe 2-quart casserole combine meat sauce and noodles. Mix shredded cheeses and sprinkle evenly over top.

3. Microwave at HIGH 3 minutes. Let stand 5 minutes. Microwave 3 minutes longer or until cheeses melt. *Makes 6 servings*

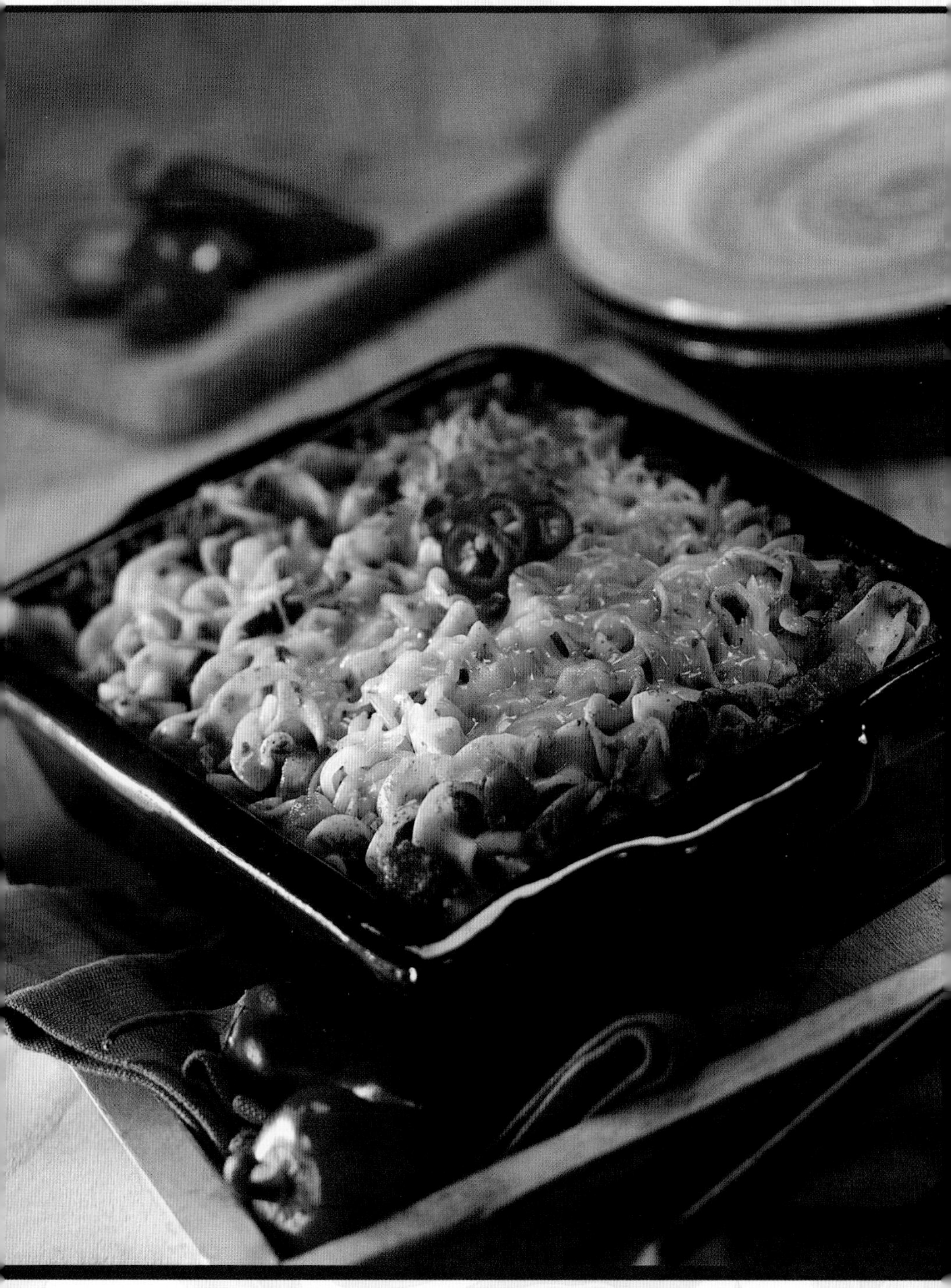

Spicy Beefy Noodles

Michigan Goulash

Diane Nemitz | Ludington, Michigan

2 tablespoons vegetable oil
1 pound ground beef or ground turkey
1 medium onion, chopped
1 large green bell pepper, seeded and diced
1 jalapeño pepper,* seeded and minced
3 ribs celery, sliced thin
1 small zucchini, sliced
1 can (8 ounces) tomato sauce
1 cup water
¾ cup barbecue sauce
1 package (8 to 10 ounces) noodles, cooked and kept warm
2 cups (8 ounces) shredded Cheddar cheese

Jalapeño peppers can sting and irritate the skin; wear rubber gloves when handling peppers and do not touch the eyes. Wash hands after handling peppers.

1. Preheat oven to 350°F. Grease 13×9-inch casserole.

2. Heat oil in large skillet, over medium-high heat. Add beef, stirring to break up meat. Add onion, bell pepper, jalapeño, celery and zucchini; cook and stir until meat is no longer pink. Add tomato sauce, water and barbecue sauce; stir to combine. Reduce heat to medium-low and simmer 20 minutes.

3. Combine meat mixture and noodles in prepared casserole; top with cheese.

4. Bake 10 to 15 minutes or until cheese melts.   *Makes 8 servings*

Barney's Colorful Casserole
Pam Brown | Davenport, Iowa

6 potatoes, peeled and sliced thin
6 to 8 carrots, peeled and sliced thin
2 onions, peeled and sliced thin
   Salt and pepper
1 can (about 46 ounces) tomato juice
1 can (about 10 ounces) chopped tomatoes with chilies
16 cooked meatballs

1. Preheat oven to 375°F. Spray 13×9-inch baking dish with nonstick cooking spray.

2. Arrange potatoes, carrots and onions in single, overlapping layer in dish. Season with salt and pepper. Heat chopped tomato juice and tomatoes in small saucepan over medium heat until hot; pour over vegetables.

3. Bake 1½ hours or until vegetables are tender. Top with meatballs and bake additional 15 minutes until browned.   *Makes 8 servings*

Cabbage Hot Dish
Mary Schulze | Janesville, Wisconsin

1 to 2 pounds ground beef
1 medium onion, chopped
2 cans (10¾ ounces each) condensed tomato soup, undiluted
1 large head cabbage, cored and shredded

1. Preheat oven to 350°F.

2. Cook beef and onion in large skillet over medium-high heat until meat is no longer pink. Drain fat from skillet. Reduce heat to low, stir in soup and simmer 5 minutes.

3. Place cabbage in a 2-quart casserole. Top with beef mixture.

4. Bake for 1½ hours or until cabbage is tender.

Makes 4 to 6 servings

Turnip Shepherd's Pie

1 pound small turnips,* peeled and cut into ½-inch cubes
1 pound lean ground turkey
⅓ cup dry bread crumbs
¼ cup chopped onion
¼ cup ketchup
1 egg
½ teaspoon salt
½ teaspoon pepper
½ teaspoon Beau Monde seasoning**
⅓ cup half-and-half
1 tablespoon butter or margarine
   Salt and black pepper
1 tablespoon chopped fresh parsley
¼ cup shredded sharp Cheddar cheese

*For Rutabaga Shepherd's Pie, use 1 pound rutabagas in place of turnips.

**Beau Monde is a seasoning salt available in most supermarkets. Celery salt may be substituted.

1. Preheat oven to 400°F. Place turnips in large saucepan; cover with water. Cover and bring to a boil; reduce heat to medium-low. Simmer 20 minutes or until fork-tender.

2. Mix turkey, crumbs, onion, ketchup, egg, salt, pepper and seasoning. Pat on bottom and side of 9-inch pie pan. Bake 20 to 30 minutes until turkey is no longer pink. Blot with paper towel to remove any drippings.

3. Drain cooked turnips. Mash turnips with electric mixer until smooth, blending in half-and-half and butter. Season with salt and pepper to taste. Fill meat shell with turnip mixture; sprinkle with parsley, then cheese. Return to oven until cheese melts. Garnish as desired. *Makes 4 main-dish servings*

Turnip Shepherd's Pie   29

Jackpot Casserole

Ann C. Port | Southborough, Massachusetts

2 tablespoons butter or olive oil
2 medium onions, chopped
2 ribs celery, chopped
1 package (8 ounces) sliced mushrooms *or* 1 can (4 ounces) sliced
    mushrooms, drained
1 to 1½ pounds ground beef
1 can (4 ounces) sliced olives, drained
1½ cups cooked rice
1 can (8 ounces) tomato sauce
Salt and pepper

1. Preheat oven to 350°F.

2. Melt butter in large skillet over medium heat. Add onions and celery; cook and stir until almost tender. Add mushrooms and cook and stir until vegetables are soft.

3. In separate medium skillet, cook beef over medium-high heat 10 minutes or until no longer pink, stirring to separate meat. Pour off fat.

4. Combine vegetable mixture, beef, olives and rice in 3- to 4-quart casserole. Add tomato sauce, salt and pepper. Mix well.

5. Cover and bake 1 hour or until heated through.

Makes 4 to 6 servings

Jambalaya

Denise J. Dempsey | Farmington, Missouri

1 pound ground beef
1 cup chopped onion
¼ cup diced green pepper
1 teaspoon salt
½ teaspoon sugar
1 can (28 ounces) tomatoes, liquid drained and reserved
¼ teaspoon dried thyme leaves
1 small bay leaf
2⅓ cups cooked rice

1. Heat large skillet over medium heat. Add beef, onion and bell pepper; cook and stir until meat is no longer pink. Drain fat.

2. Add enough water to reserved tomato liquid to make 1½ cups. Add liquid, tomatoes, salt, sugar, thyme and bay leaf to skillet. Simmer 5 minutes.

3. Stir in rice; cover and simmer 5 minutes longer. Remove and discard bay leaf before serving. *Makes 4 to 6 servings*

FROM
THE PANTRY

Rainbow Casserole
Barbara Davis | Lake Geneva, Wisconsin

5 potatoes, peeled and cut into thin slices
1 pound ground beef
1 onion, peeled, halved and cut into thin slices
   Salt and pepper
1 can (about 28 ounces) stewed tomatoes, drained, juice reserved
1 cup frozen peas *or* 1 can (about 6 ounces) peas

1. Preheat oven to 350°F. Spray 3-quart casserole with nonstick cooking spray.

2. Boil potatoes in salted water in large saucepan until almost tender. Drain and reserve. Meanwhile, cook and stir ground beef in medium skillet until no longer pink. Drain fat.

3. Layer ½ of ground beef, ½ of potatoes, ½ of onions, salt and pepper, ½ of tomatoes and ½ of peas. Repeat layers. Add reserved tomato juice.

4. Bake, covered, about 40 minutes or until most of liquid is absorbed. *Makes 4 to 6 servings*

Crab-Artichoke Casserole

Marilyn Pocius | Oak Park, Illinois

8 ounces uncooked shell-shaped pasta
2 tablespoons butter
6 green onions, chopped
2 tablespoons all purpose flour
1 cup half-and-half
1 teaspoon dry mustard
½ teaspoon ground red pepper
   Salt and black pepper
½ cup shredded Swiss cheese, divided
1 can (about 14 ounces) artichoke hearts in water, drained and cut
   into bite-size pieces
1 package (about 8 ounces) imitation crabmeat chunks

1. Preheat oven to 350°F. Grease 2-quart casserole. Cook pasta in large saucepan of salted boiling water; drain and reserve.

2. Heat butter in large saucepan over medium heat; add green onions. Cook and stir about 2 minutes. Add flour; cook and stir 2 minutes more. Gradually add half-and-half, whisking constantly until mixture begins to thicken. Whisk in mustard, red pepper and season with salt and black pepper. Remove from heat and stir in ¼ cup Swiss cheese until melted.

3. Combine artichokes, imitation crab and pasta in prepared casserole. Add sauce mixture and stir well. Top with remaining ¼ cup cheese. Bake about 40 minutes until hot, bubbly and lightly browned.

Makes 6 servings

Marilyn says: This can also be baked in individual dishes. You'll want to reduce cooking time to about 20 minutes.

Crab-Artichoke Casserole

Denver Spoonbread

3 tablespoons butter, divided
2 tablespoons grated Parmesan cheese
½ cup chopped onion
¼ cup chopped green bell pepper
¼ cup chopped red bell pepper
2½ cups milk
1 cup yellow cornmeal
1 teaspoon salt
1½ cups (6 ounces) shredded Cheddar cheese
4 eggs, separated*

Egg whites must be free from any yolk to reach proper volume when beaten.

1. Preheat oven to 350°F.

2. Grease 1½-quart soufflé dish with 1 tablespoon butter. Sprinkle bottom and side of dish evenly with Parmesan cheese.

3. Melt remaining 2 tablespoons butter in medium, heavy saucepan over medium heat. Add onion and bell peppers; cook 5 to 7 minutes or until tender, stirring occasionally. Transfer mixture to small bowl; set aside.

4. Combine milk, cornmeal and salt in same saucepan. Bring to a boil over high heat. Reduce heat to medium; cook and stir 5 minutes or until mixture thickens. Remove from heat. Stir in Cheddar cheese until cheese is melted. Stir in onion mixture.

5. Beat egg whites in clean large bowl using clean beaters with electric mixer at high speed until stiff but not dry; set aside.

6. Beat egg yolks in separate large bowl. Stir into cornmeal mixture. Stir ⅓ of egg whites into cornmeal mixture. Fold remaining egg whites into cornmeal mixture until evenly incorporated. Pour into prepared soufflé dish.

7. Bake about 50 minutes or until puffed and golden brown. Serve immediately. Garnish, if desired. *Makes 6 servings*

Ham & Egg Enchiladas

2 tablespoons butter or margarine
1 small red bell pepper, chopped
3 green onions with tops, sliced
½ cup diced ham
8 eggs
8 (7- to 8-inch) flour tortillas
2 cups (8 ounces) shredded Colby-Jack cheese or Pepper-Jack
   cheese, divided
1 can (10 ounces) enchilada sauce
½ cup prepared salsa
   Sliced avocado, fresh cilantro and red pepper slices for garnish

1. Preheat oven to 350°F.

2. Melt butter in large nonstick skillet over medium heat. Add bell
pepper and onions; cook and stir 2 minutes. Add ham; cook and stir
1 minute.

3. Lightly beat eggs with wire whisk in medium bowl. Add eggs to
skillet; cook until eggs are set, but still soft, stirring occasionally.

4. Spoon about ⅓ cup egg mixture evenly down center of each tortilla;
top with 1 tablespoon cheese. Roll tortillas up and place seam side
down in shallow 11×7-inch baking dish.

5. Combine enchilada sauce and salsa in small bowl; pour evenly over
enchiladas.

6. Cover enchiladas with foil; bake 20 minutes. Uncover; sprinkle
with remaining cheese. Continue baking 10 minutes or until enchiladas
are hot and cheese is melted. Garnish, if desired. Serve immediately.

Makes 4 servings

Ham and Egg Enchiladas 39

Vegetarian Paella

1 tablespoon olive oil
1 medium onion, chopped
1 serrano pepper,* finely chopped
1 red bell pepper, diced
1 green bell pepper, diced
3 cloves garlic, minced
½ teaspoon saffron threads, crushed
½ teaspoon paprika
1 cup uncooked long-grain white rice
3 cups water
1 can (15 ounces) chick-peas, rinsed and drained
1 can (14 ounces) artichoke hearts in water, drained and cut into
    halves
1 cup frozen green peas
1½ teaspoons grated lemon peel

Serrano peppers can sting and irritate the skin; wear rubber gloves when handling peppers and do not touch eyes. Wash hands after handling peppers.

1. Preheat oven to 375°F. Heat oil in large paella pan or heavy, ovenproof skillet over medium-high heat. Add onion, serrano pepper and bell peppers; cook and stir about 7 minutes.

2. Add garlic, saffron and paprika; cook 3 minutes. Add rice; cook and stir 1 minute. Add water, chick-peas, artichoke hearts, green peas and lemon peel; mix well.

3. Cover and bake 25 minutes or until rice is tender. Garnish with fresh bay leaves and lemon slices, if desired.   *Makes 6 servings*

Aunt Marilyn's
Cinnamon French Toast Casserole
Marilyn Gordon | Chicago, Illinois

1 large loaf French Bread, cut into 1½-inch slices
3½ cups milk
9 eggs
1½ cups sugar, divided
1 tablespoon vanilla
½ teaspoon salt
6 to 8 medium cooking apples, such as McIntosh or Cortland, peeled and sliced
1 teaspoon cinnamon
½ teaspoon nutmeg

1. Squeeze bread slices into greased 13×9-inch glass baking dish or casserole.

2. Whisk milk, eggs, 1 cup sugar, vanilla and salt in large bowl 30 seconds until well combined. Pour ½ of mixture over bread.

3. Layer apple slices on top. Pour remaining ½ of egg mixture over apples.

4. Mix remaining ½ cup sugar, cinnamon and nutmeg in small bowl; sprinkle over dish. Cover and refrigerate overnight.

5. Bake, uncovered, at 350°F 1 hour until heated through and eggs are set.

Makes 6 to 8 servings

Crunchy Top & Flaky Bottom Broccoli Casserole

Gloria Herdman | Pomeroy, Ohio

2 cans (8 ounces each) refrigerated crescent roll dough
1 package (16 ounces) frozen chopped broccoli
2 cups (8 ounces) shredded mozzarella cheese, divided
1½ cups French fried onions, coarsely crushed and divided
1 can (10¾ ounces) condensed cream of mushroom soup, undiluted
2 cans (5 ounces each) lean ham, drained and flaked
½ cup mayonnaise
2 eggs, beaten
2 tablespoons Dijon mustard
1 tablespoon prepared horseradish
1 jar (2 ounces) chopped pimientos, drained
1 teaspoon finely chopped fresh parsley

1. Preheat oven to 375°F. Butter bottom of 13×9-inch baking dish. Unroll cans of dough; do not separate. Press dough onto bottom of prepared baking dish, sealing all seams. Bake 7 minutes; remove from oven and set aside.

2. Combine broccoli, 1 cup cheese, ½ cup onions, soup, ham, mayonnaise, eggs, mustard and horseradish. Spread evenly over crust. Top with remaining 1 cup onions, 1 cup cheese, pimientos and parsley.

3. Bake for 20 to 25 minutes or until set. Cool 10 minutes before serving. *Makes 8 servings*

Chicken, Asparagus & Mushroom Bake

Marilyn Pocius | Oak Park, Illinois

1 tablespoon butter
1 tablespoon olive oil
2 boneless skinless chicken breasts (about ½ pound), cut into bite-size pieces
2 cloves garlic, minced
2 cups sliced asparagus
1 cup sliced mushrooms
  Freshly ground black pepper
1 package (about 6 ounces) cornbread stuffing mix
¼ cup white wine (optional)
1 can (about 14 ounces) reduced-sodium chicken broth
1 can (14 ½ ounces) condensed cream of asparagus or cream of chicken soup, undiluted (reduced-sodium preferred)

1. Preheat oven to 350°F. Heat butter and oil in large skillet. Cook and stir chicken and garlic about 3 minutes over medium-high heat until chicken is no longer pink. Add mushrooms, cook and stir 2 minutes more. Add asparagus; cook and stir about five minutes until vegetables soften slightly. Season with pepper.

2. Transfer mixture to 2½ quart casserole. Add stuffing mix to casserole.

3. Add wine to skillet, if desired; cook and stir 1 minute over medium high heat, scraping up any browned bits from bottom of skillet. Add broth and soup; cook and stir to combine.

4. Pour broth mixture into casserole. Mix contents well. Bake, uncovered, about 35 minutes or until heated through and lightly browned. *Makes 6 servings*

Marilyn says: This is a good way to stretch a little leftover chicken into an easy and tasty dinner.

Chicken, Asparagus & Mushroom Bake

Broccoli-Fish Roll-Ups

1 can (10¾ ounces) condensed cream of broccoli soup, undiluted
½ cup fat-free (skim) milk
2 cups seasoned stuffing crumbs
¾ pound flounder (4 medium pieces)
1 box (10 ounces) frozen broccoli spears, thawed
  Paprika

1. Preheat oven to 375°F. Grease 9×9-inch baking dish. Combine soup and milk in medium bowl. Set aside ½ cup soup mixture.

2. Combine stuffing crumbs and remaining soup mixture. Pat into prepared pan.

3. Place fish on clean work surface. Arrange 1 broccoli spear across narrow end of fish. Starting at narrow end, gently roll up fish. Place over stuffing mixture, seam side down. Repeat with remaining fish and broccoli.

4. Arrange any remaining broccoli spears over stuffing mixture. Spoon reserved ½ cup soup mixture over broccoli-fish rollups. Sprinkle with paprika.

5. Bake 20 minutes or until fish flakes easily when tested with fork.

Makes 4 servings

Variation: Asparagus spears and cream of asparagus soup may be substituted for broccoli spears and cream of broccoli soup.

Broccoli-Fish Roll-Ups   47

New England Baked Beans

½ pound dried navy beans
¼ pound salt pork, trimmed
  Water
1 small onion, chopped
2 cloves garlic, minced
3 tablespoons packed brown sugar
3 tablespoons maple syrup
3 tablespoons unsulphured molasses
½ teaspoon salt
½ teaspoon dry mustard
⅛ teaspoon black pepper
½ bay leaf
⅓ cup canned diced tomatoes, well drained

1. Rinse beans thoroughly in colander under cold running water. Place in large bowl; cover with 4 inches water. Let stand at least 8 hours, then rinse and drain.

2. Cut pork into 4 (¼-inch-thick) slices. Score pork with tip of sharp knife, taking care not to cut completely through pork; set aside.

3. Bring 3 cups water to a boil in 1-quart saucepan. Place pork in water; boil 1 minute. Remove from saucepan to medium plate. Slice and set aside.

4. Place beans in heavy, 3-quart saucepan. Cover beans with 2 inches cold water. Bring beans to a boil over high heat. Reduce heat to low; simmer, covered, 30 to 35 minutes until tender. Drain; reserve liquid.

5. Preheat oven to 350°F. Line bottom of large casserole with ½ of pork slices. Spoon beans over pork slices.

6. Place 2 cups reserved bean liquid into 1½-quart saucepan. Bring to a boil over high heat. Add onion, garlic, brown sugar, maple syrup, molasses, salt, mustard, pepper and bay leaf; simmer 2 minutes. Stir in tomatoes; cook 1 minute. Pour onion mixture over beans in casserole. Top with remaining pork slices.

7. Cover casserole with foil. Bake 2½ hours. Remove cover; bake 30 minutes or until thickened. Skim fat from surface.

8. Discard pork slices and bay leaf before serving. Garnish with fresh parsley, if desired. *Makes 4 to 6 servings*

New England Baked Beans 49

Tuna Pot Pie

1 tablespoon butter
1 small onion, chopped
1 can (10¾ ounces) condensed cream of potato soup, undiluted
¼ cup milk
½ teaspoon dried thyme leaves
¼ teaspoon salt
⅛ teaspoon black pepper
2 cans (6 ounces each) albacore tuna in water, drained
1 package (16 ounces) frozen vegetable medley, such as broccoli,
    green beans, carrots and red peppers, thawed
2 tablespoons chopped fresh parsley
1 can (8 ounces) refrigerated crescent roll dough

1. Preheat oven to 350°F. Spray 11×7-inch baking dish with nonstick cooking spray.

2. Melt butter in large skillet over medium heat. Add onion; cook and stir 2 minutes or until onion is tender. Add soup, milk, thyme, salt and pepper; cook and stir 3 to 4 minutes or until thick and bubbly. Stir in tuna, vegetables and parsley. Pour mixture into prepared dish.

3. Unroll crescent roll dough and divide into triangles. Place triangles over tuna filling without overlapping dough. Bake, uncovered, 20 minutes or until triangles are golden brown. Let stand 5 minutes before serving. *Makes 6 servings*

Home Cook's HINT

Experiment with different vegetable combinations and create an exciting recipe every time. Just substitute a new medley for the one listed and enjoy the results.

Tuna Pot Pie

Baked Tomato Risotto

1 jar (28 ounces) spaghetti sauce
2 cups sliced zucchini
1 can (14 ounces) chicken broth
1 cup arborio rice
1 can (4 ounces) sliced mushrooms
2 cups (8 ounces) shredded mozzarella cheese

1. Preheat oven to 350°F. Spray 3-quart casserole with nonstick cooking spray.

2. Combine spaghetti sauce, zucchini, broth, rice and mushrooms in prepared dish.

3. Bake, covered, 30 minutes. Remove from oven and stir casserole. Cover and bake 15 to 20 minutes more or until rice is tender. Remove from oven; sprinkle evenly with cheese. Bake, uncovered, 5 minutes or until cheese is melted. *Makes 6 servings*

Potato Nugget Casserole
Tracey Lyn Franklin | Euless, Texas

2 pounds frozen potato nuggets
1 can (10¾ ounces) condensed cream of celery soup, undiluted
1 can (10¾ ounces) condensed cream of mushroom soup, undiluted
1 can (10¾ ounces) condensed Cheddar cheese soup, undiluted
1 can (about 5 ounces) evaporated milk
2 cups (8 ounces) shredded mozzarella cheese
2 cups (8 ounces) shredded Cheddar cheese

1. Preheat oven to 350°F. Pour potatoes into 13×9-inch casserole; set aside.

2. Mix soups and evaporated milk in large saucepan. Bring to a boil, stirring occasionally. Pour over potatoes and mix until well-combined.

3. Bake 45 minutes. Remove from oven; sprinkle cheeses evenly over casserole. Bake 5 minutes more or until cheeses melt.

Makes 10 servings

Baked Tomato Risotto 53

Wild Rice & Chicken Casserole

Andrée Tracey | St. Louis Park, Minnesota

1 package (6 ounces) long grain & wild rice mix
2 tablespoons butter
½ cup chopped onion
½ cup chopped celery
1 can (10¾ ounces) condensed cream of mushroom soup, undiluted
½ cup sour cream
⅓ cup dry white wine
½ teaspoon curry powder
2 cups cooked cubed chicken

1. Preheat oven to 350°F.

2. Prepare rice mix according to package directions. Melt butter in large skillet over medium heat; cook and stir onion and celery until tender. Stir in soup, sour cream, wine and curry powder. Stir in chicken and rice.

3. Transfer to 2-quart casserole. Bake 40 minutes or until heated through. Stir before serving.   *Makes 4 to 6 servings*

Andrée says: This casserole tastes even better reheated the next day and also freezes well. I often prepare a batch for my elderly father to stock his freezer.

Stroganoff Casserole

Karen Tellier | Cumberland, Rhode Island

1 package (16 ounces) egg noodles
2 cans (10¾ ounces each) condensed fat-free cream of mushroom
   soup, undiluted
1 container (8 ounces) reduced-fat sour cream
½ cup milk
1 pound lean ground beef
2 cans (6 ounces each) sliced mushrooms, undrained
1 package (8 ounces) reduced-fat cream cheese
1 package (about 1 ounce) gravy mix

1. Preheat oven to 350°F. Cook noodles according to package directions in 4-quart Dutch oven. Drain and return to pan.

2. Add mushroom soup, sour cream and milk to noodles; stir to combine. Cover and keep warm.

3. Brown ground beef in large skillet over medium-high heat until no longer pink, stirring to separate. Drain fat from skillet.

4. Add mushrooms, cream cheese and gravy mix to beef; blend well. Combine with noodle mixture in Dutch oven; stir until well blended.

5. Bake 30 minutes or until heated through.   *Makes 8 servings*

CHICKEN
IN EVERY POT

Escalloped Chicken
Billie Olofson | Des Moines, Iowa

10 slices white bread, cubed
1½ cups cracker or dry bread crumbs, divided
4 cups cubed cooked chicken
3 cups chicken broth
1 cup chopped onion
1 cup chopped celery
1 can (8 ounces) sliced mushrooms, drained
1 jar (about 4 ounces) pimientos, diced
3 eggs, lightly beaten
Salt and pepper
1 tablespoon margarine

1. Preheat oven to 350°F.

2. Combine bread cubes and 1 cup cracker crumbs in large mixing bowl. Add chicken, broth, onion, celery, mushrooms, pimientos and eggs; mix well. Season with salt and pepper; spoon into 2½-quart casserole.

3. Melt margarine in small saucepan. Add remaining ½ cup cracker crumbs and brown, stirring occasionally. Sprinkle crumbs over casserole.

4. Bake 1 hour or until hot and bubbly.   *Makes 6 servings*

Chicken Bourguignonne

4 pounds boneless skinless chicken thighs and breasts
Flour
1 to 2 tablespoons vegetable oil
2 cups fat-free reduced-sodium chicken broth
2 cups dry white wine or chicken broth
1 pound whole baby carrots
1/4 cup tomato paste
4 cloves garlic, minced
1/2 teaspoon dried thyme leaves
2 bay leaves
1/4 teaspoon salt
1/4 teaspoon black pepper
8 ounces fresh or thawed frozen pearl onions
8 ounces whole medium mushrooms
2 cups hot cooked white rice
2 cups hot cooked wild rice
1/4 cup minced fresh parsley

1. Preheat oven to 325°F. Coat chicken very lightly with flour. Heat
1 tablespoon oil in Dutch oven or large ovenproof skillet over medium
heat. Cook chicken in batches 10 to 15 minutes or until browned on all
sides, adding additional oil as needed. Drain fat.

2. Add broth, wine, carrots, tomato paste, garlic, thyme, bay leaves,
salt and pepper to Dutch oven; heat to a boil. Cover; transfer to oven.
Bake 1 hour. Add onions and mushrooms. Uncover; bake about
35 minutes or until vegetables are tender, chicken is no longer pink in
center and juices run clear. Remove and discard bay leaves. Combine
white and wild rice; serve with chicken. Sprinkle with parsley.

Makes 8 servings

Chicken Bourguignonne   59

Chicken Cassoulet

Marilyn Pocius | Oak Park, Illinois

4 slices bacon
¼ cup all-purpose flour
  Salt and pepper
1¾ pounds chicken pieces
  2 cooked chicken sausages, cut into ¼-inch pieces
  1 onion, chopped
  2 cloves garlic, finely chopped
1½ cups diced red and green bell pepper (2 small bell peppers)
  Olive oil, as needed
  2 cans (about 15 ounces each) white beans, such as Great Northern,
    drained and rinsed
  1 teaspoon dried thyme leaves
½ cup white wine (optional)
  Salt and pepper

1. Preheat oven to 350°F. Cook bacon in large skillet over medium-high heat until crisp. Remove and drain on paper towels. Cut into 1-inch pieces.

2. Leave about 2 tablespoons fat in skillet; pour off excess. Place flour in shallow bowl, season with salt and pepper. Dip chicken pieces in flour, shake off excess and brown in batches over medium-high heat in skillet. Remove and reserve. Lightly brown sausage in same skillet. Remove and reserve.

3. Add onions, bell pepper, garlic and thyme to skillet. Cook and stir over medium heat about 5 minutes until softened. Add olive oil as needed to prevent sticking. Pour into 13×9-inch baking dish. Add beans and stir to combine. Top with chicken, sausages and bacon. If desired, add wine to skillet; cook and stir over medium heat, scraping up brown bits; pour over casserole.

4. Cover and bake 40 minutes. Uncover and bake 15 minutes more or until chicken is no longer pink in center. *Makes 6 servings*

Saffron Chicken & Vegetables

Brenda Melancon | Bay St. Louis, Mississippi

2 tablespoons vegetable oil
6 bone-in chicken thighs, skinned
1 bag (16 ounces) frozen mixed vegetables, such as broccoli, red
    peppers, mushrooms and onions, thawed
1 can (14½ ounces) roasted garlic flavor chicken broth
1 can (10¾ ounces) condensed cream of chicken soup, undiluted
1 can (10¾ ounces) condensed cream of mushroom soup, undiluted
1 package (about 8 ounces) saffron yellow rice mix with seasonings
½ cup water
½ teaspoon salt
1 teaspoon paprika (optional)

1. Preheat oven to 350°F. Spray 3-quart casserole with nonstick cooking spray; set aside.

2. Heat oil in large skillet over medium heat. Add chicken and brown thoroughly, about 10 minutes.

3. Meanwhile, combine vegetables, chicken broth, soup, rice mix with seasonings, water and salt in large bowl. Place mixture in prepared casserole. Top with chicken. Sprinkle with paprika, if desired. Cover and bake 1½ hours until chicken is no longer pink in center.

Makes 6 servings

Home Cook's HINT

To brown chicken easily make sure it is dry and never crowd the pan. It's better to brown in batches, removing pieces as they are done. Crowding causes the meat to steam rather than brown. Avoid high heat for browning chicken as it can make the meat close to the surface become stringy.

Saffron Chicken & Vegetables 63

Spicy Chicken Casserole with Cornbread

Kathy Rouse | Fayetteville, North Carolina

2 tablespoons olive oil
4 skinless boneless chicken breasts, cut into bite-size pieces
1 envelope (about 1 ounce) taco seasoning
1 can (about 15 ounces) black beans, drained and rinsed
1 can (14½ ounces) diced tomatoes, drained
1 can (about 10 ounces) Mexican-style corn, drained
1 can (about 4 ounces) diced chilies, drained
½ cup mild salsa
1 box (about 8½ ounces) cornbread mix, plus ingredients for mix
½ cup Cheddar cheese
¼ cup chopped red bell pepper

1. Heat oil in large skillet over medium heat. Cook chicken until no longer pink. Sprinkle taco seasoning over chicken. Add black beans, tomatoes, corn, chilies and salsa; stir to combine well. Transfer to 2-quart casserole sprayed with nonstick cooking spray.

2. Prepare cornbread mix according to package directions, adding bell pepper and cheese, *but do not bake.* Pour over chicken and bean mixture.

3. Bake at 350°F for 30 minutes or until cornbread is golden brown.

Makes 4 to 6 servings

Home Cook's HINT

Thoroughly wash cutting surfaces, utensils and your hands with hot soapy water after coming in contact with uncooked chicken. This eliminates the risk of contaminating other foods with the salmonella bacteria that is often present in raw chicken. Salmonella is killed during cooking.

Spicy Chicken Casserole with Cornbread

Chicken Marsala

4 cups (6 ounces) uncooked broad egg noodles
½ cup Italian-seasoned dry bread crumbs
1 teaspoon dried basil leaves
1 egg
1 teaspoon water
4 boneless skinless chicken breasts
3 tablespoons olive oil, divided
¾ cup chopped onion
8 ounces cremini or button mushrooms, sliced
3 cloves garlic, minced
3 tablespoons all-purpose flour
1 can (14½ ounces) chicken broth
½ cup dry marsala wine
¾ teaspoon salt
¼ teaspoon black pepper
Chopped fresh parsley (optional)

1. Preheat oven to 375°F. Spray 11×7-inch baking dish with nonstick cooking spray.

2. Cook noodles according to package directions until al dente. Drain and place in prepared dish.

3. Meanwhile, combine bread crumbs and basil on shallow plate or pie plate. Beat egg with water on another shallow plate or pie plate. Dip chicken in egg mixture, letting excess drip off. Roll in crumb mixture, patting to coat.

4. Heat 2 tablespoons oil in large skillet over medium-high heat until hot. Cook chicken 3 minutes per side or until browned. Transfer to clean plate; set aside.

5. Heat remaining 1 tablespoon oil in same skillet over medium heat. Add onion; cook and stir 5 minutes. Add mushrooms and garlic; cook and stir 3 minutes. Sprinkle mushroom mixture with flour; cook and stir 1 minute. Add broth, wine, salt and pepper; bring to a boil over high heat. Cook and stir 5 minutes or until sauce thickens.

6. Reserve ½ cup sauce. Pour remaining sauce over noodles; stir until noodles are well coated. Place chicken on top of noodles. Spoon reserved sauce over chicken.

7. Bake, uncovered, about 20 minutes or until chicken is no longer pink in center and sauce is hot and bubbly. Sprinkle with parsley, if desired.

Makes 4 servings

Home Cook's HINT

Marsala is Italy's most famous fortified wine. Its rich, smoky flavor makes it a frequent (and delicious) cooking ingredient.

Chicken Marsala

Chicken Divan Casserole

Susan Richardson | Libertyville, Illinois

1 cup uncooked rice
1 cup coarsely shredded carrots*
  Nonstick cooking spray
4 boneless skinless chicken breasts
2 tablespoons butter or margarine
3 tablespoons all-purpose flour
¼ teaspoon salt
  Black pepper to taste
1 cup fat-free chicken broth
½ cup milk or half-and-half
¼ cup white wine
⅓ cup plus 2 tablespoons grated Parmesan cheese, divided
1 pound frozen broccoli florets

Coarsely shredded carrots are available in the produce section of many large supermarkets.

1. Preheat oven to 350°F. Lightly grease 12×8-inch baking dish.

2. Prepare rice according to package directions. Stir in carrots. Spread mixture into prepared baking dish.

3. Spray large skillet with cooking spray. Heat over medium-high heat. Brown chicken breasts about 2 minutes on each side. Arrange over rice.

4. To prepare sauce, melt butter in 2-quart saucepan over medium heat. Whisk in flour, salt and pepper; cook and stir 1 minute. Gradually whisk in broth and milk. Cook and stir until mixture comes to a boil. Reduce heat; simmer for 2 minutes. Stir in wine. Remove from heat. Stir in ⅓ cup cheese.

5. Arrange broccoli around chicken. Pour sauce over chicken and broccoli. Sprinkle remaining 2 tablespoons cheese over chicken. Bake 10 to 15 minutes or until chicken is no longer pink in center and broccoli is hot. *Makes 6 servings*

Apple Curry Chicken

    4 boneless skinless chicken breasts
    1 cup apple juice, divided
    ¼ teaspoon salt
      Dash black pepper
  1½ cups plain croutons
    1 medium apple, chopped
    1 medium onion, chopped
    ¼ cup raisins
    2 teaspoons brown sugar
    1 teaspoon curry powder
    ¾ teaspoon poultry seasoning
    ⅛ teaspoon garlic powder
    2 apple slices and fresh thyme sprigs for garnish (optional)

1. Preheat oven to 350°F. Lightly grease 2-quart round baking dish.

2. Arrange chicken breasts in single layer in prepared dish.

3. Combine ¼ cup apple juice, salt and pepper in small bowl. Brush juice mixture over chicken.

4. Combine croutons, apple, onion, raisins, brown sugar, curry, poultry seasoning and garlic powder in large bowl. Toss with remaining ¾ cup apple juice.

5. Spread crouton mixture over chicken. Cover with foil; bake 45 minutes or until chicken is tender and no longer pink in center. Garnish, if desired.   *Makes 4 servings*

Coq au Vin

½ cup all-purpose flour
1¼ teaspoons salt
¾ teaspoon black pepper
3½ pounds chicken pieces
2 tablespoons margarine or butter
8 ounces mushrooms, cut in half if large
4 cloves garlic, minced
¾ cup chicken broth
¾ cup dry red wine
2 teaspoons dried thyme leaves
1½ pounds red potatoes, quartered
2 cups frozen pearl onions (about 8 ounces)
Chopped fresh parsley (optional)

1. Preheat oven to 350°F.

2. Combine flour, salt and pepper in large resealable plastic food storage bag or paper bag. Add chicken, two pieces at a time, and seal bag. Shake to coat chicken; remove chicken and set aside. Repeat with remaining pieces. Reserve remaining flour mixture.

3. Melt margarine in ovenproof Dutch oven over medium-high heat. Arrange chicken in single layer in Dutch oven and cook 3 minutes per side or until browned. Transfer to plate; set aside. Repeat with remaining pieces.

4. Add mushrooms and garlic to Dutch oven; cook and stir 2 minutes. Sprinkle reserved flour mixture over mushroom mixture; cook and stir 1 minute. Add broth, wine and thyme; bring to a boil over high heat, stirring to scrape up browned bits on bottom of Dutch oven. Add potatoes and onions; return to a boil. Remove from heat and place chicken in Dutch oven, partially covering chicken with broth mixture.

5. Bake, covered, about 45 minutes or until chicken is no longer pink in centers, potatoes are tender and sauce is slightly thickened. Transfer chicken and vegetables to shallow bowls. Spoon sauce over chicken and vegetables. Sprinkle with parsley, if desired.

Makes 4 to 6 servings

Chicken Pot Pie

1½ pounds chicken pieces, skinned
1 cup chicken broth
½ teaspoon salt
¼ teaspoon black pepper
1 to 1½ cups reduced-fat (2%) milk
3 tablespoons butter
1 medium onion, chopped
1 cup sliced celery
⅓ cup all-purpose flour
2 cups frozen mixed vegetables (broccoli, carrots and cauliflower combination), thawed
1 tablespoon chopped fresh parsley *or* 1 teaspoon dried parsley
½ teaspoon dried thyme leaves
1 (9-inch) refrigerated pastry crust
1 egg, lightly beaten

1. Combine chicken, chicken broth, salt and pepper in large saucepan over medium-high heat. Bring to a boil. Reduce heat to low. Cover; simmer 30 minutes or until juices run clear.

2. Remove chicken and let cool. Pour remaining chicken broth mixture into glass measure. Let stand; spoon off fat. Add enough milk to broth mixture to equal 2½ cups. Remove chicken from bones and cut into ½-inch pieces.

3. Melt butter in same saucepan over medium heat. Add onion and celery. Cook and stir 3 minutes. Stir in flour until well blended. Gradually stir in broth mixture. Cook, stirring constantly, until sauce thickens and boils. Add chicken, vegetables, parsley and thyme. Pour into 1½-quart deep casserole.

4. Preheat oven to 400°F. Roll out pastry crust 1 inch larger than diameter of casserole on lightly floured surface. Cut slits to vent and place pastry on top of casserole. Cut away extra pastry and flute edges. Reroll scraps to cut into decorative designs. Place on top of pastry; brush with beaten egg. Bake about 30 minutes until crust is golden brown and filling is bubbling. *Makes about 4 servings*

Chicken, Stuffing & Green Bean Bake

1 package (7 ounces) cubed herb-seasoned stuffing
4 sheets (18×12 inches) heavy-duty foil, lightly sprayed with
    nonstick cooking spray
½ cup chicken broth
3 cups frozen cut green beans
4 boneless skinless chicken breasts
1 cup chicken gravy
⅛ teaspoon black pepper
    Additional chicken gravy, heated (optional)

1. Preheat oven to 450°F.

2. Place a quarter of stuffing (1 scant cup) on one sheet of foil. Pour 2 tablespoons chicken broth over stuffing. Top stuffing with ¾ cup green beans. Place one chicken breast on top of beans. Combine gravy and pepper; pour ¼ cup over chicken.

3. Double fold sides and ends of foil to seal packets, leaving head space for heat circulation. Repeat with remaining stuffing, beans, chicken and gravy mixture to make three more packets. Place packets on baking sheet.

4. Bake 20 minutes or until chicken is no longer pink in center. Remove from oven. Carefully open one end of each packet to allow steam to escape. Open packets and transfer contents to serving plates. Serve with additional gravy, if desired. *Makes 4 servings*

Home Cook's HINT

When cooking in foil, wrap food with the shiny side of the foil on the outside. This helps prevent over-browning. Be very careful when handling the cooked packets as they are extremely hot.

Chicken, Stuffing & Green Bean Bake 77

Sweet & Sour Chicken and Rice

1 pound chicken tenders
1 can (8 ounces) pineapple chunks, drained and juice reserved
1 cup uncooked rice
2 carrots, thinly sliced
1 green bell pepper, cut into 1-inch pieces
1 large onion, chopped
3 cloves garlic, minced
1 can (14½ ounces) reduced-sodium chicken broth
⅓ cup soy sauce
3 tablespoons sugar
3 tablespoons apple cider vinegar
1 tablespoon sesame oil
1½ teaspoons ground ginger
¼ cup chopped peanuts (optional)
Chopped fresh cilantro (optional)

1. Preheat oven to 350°F. Spray 13×9-inch baking dish with nonstick cooking spray.

2. Combine chicken, pineapple, rice, carrots, bell pepper, onion and garlic in prepared dish.

3. Place broth, reserved pineapple juice, soy sauce, sugar, vinegar, sesame oil and ginger in small saucepan; bring to a boil over high heat. Remove from heat and pour over chicken mixture.

4. Cover tightly with foil and bake 40 to 50 minutes or until chicken is no longer pink in center and rice is tender. Sprinkle with peanuts and cilantro, if desired. *Makes 6 servings*

Sweet & Sour Chicken and Rice

Cheesy Chicken Roll-Ups

¼ cup butter
1 medium onion, diced
4 ounces fresh mushrooms, sliced
3 boneless skinless chicken breasts, cut into bite-sized pieces
¾ cup dry white wine
½ teaspoon dried tarragon leaves
½ teaspoon salt
½ teaspoon black pepper
6 lasagna noodles, cooked, drained
1 package (8 ounces) cream cheese, softened, cubed
1½ cups (6 ounces) shredded Swiss cheese, divided
1 cup (4 ounces) shredded Muenster cheese, divided
½ cup heavy cream
½ cup sour cream
3 tablespoons sliced almonds, toasted*
Chopped fresh parsley (optional)

To toast almonds, spread in single layer on baking sheet. Bake in preheated 350°F oven 8 to 10 minutes or until golden brown, stirring frequently.

1. Preheat oven to 325°F. Grease 13×9-inch baking pan; set aside.

2. Melt butter in large skillet over medium-high heat. Add onion and mushrooms; cook and stir until tender. Add chicken, wine, tarragon, salt and pepper; bring to a boil over high heat. Reduce heat to low. Simmer 10 minutes.

3. Cut lasagna noodles in half lengthwise. Curl each half into a circle; arrange in prepared pan. With slotted spoon, fill center of lasagna rings with chicken mixture, reserving liquid in skillet.

4. To remaining liquid in skillet, add cream cheese, heavy cream, sour cream, ¾ cup Swiss cheese and ½ cup Muenster cheese. Cook and stir over medium-low heat until cheese melts. Do not boil. Pour over lasagna rings. Sprinkle remaining cheeses and almonds on top.

5. Bake 35 minutes or until bubbly. Sprinkle with parsley, if desired.

Makes 6 servings

Cheesy Chicken Roll-Ups

Chicken Primavera Buffet

12 ounces uncooked thin spaghetti
¼ cup prepared pesto
¼ cup fat-free Italian salad dressing
½ teaspoon red pepper flakes
2 cups water
1 cup thinly sliced carrots
1 cup broccoli florets
1 cup snow peas
1 can (4 ounces) sliced water chestnuts, drained
  Nonstick cooking spray
8 boneless skinless chicken breast halves

1. Preheat oven to 350°F. Spray 13×9-inch baking dish with nonstick cooking spray. Cook pasta according to package directions. Drain and rinse under cold water until pasta is cool; drain well. Place in large bowl; set aside.

2. Combine pesto, Italian dressing and red pepper flakes in small bowl. Reserve 1 tablespoon pesto mixture. Add remaining pesto mixture to pasta; toss to coat well.

3. In large saucepan, bring water to a boil over high heat. Add carrots, broccoli and snow peas; cook 3 minutes. Drain vegetables. Add water chestnuts and vegetables to pasta; toss to blend well. Transfer pasta and vegetables to prepared pan.

4. Spray large nonstick skillet with cooking spray; heat over medium heat until hot. Add chicken; cook until browned on both sides. Cover; cook 10 minutes or until no longer pink in center and juices run clear. Place chicken on pasta and vegetables. Pour juices from skillet over chicken. Spread reserved pesto mixture over chicken. Bake 45 minutes or until heated through. *Makes 8 servings*

Chicken Primavera Buffet   83

Italian Chicken My Way
Debbie Auterson | Rio, California

    ½ cup dry breadcrumbs
    ¼ cup grated Parmesan cheese
    6 skinless boneless chicken breasts, cut in half lengthwise
    4 tablespoons (½ stick) of margarine
    1 package (10 ounces) frozen chopped broccoli, thawed
    1 teaspoon garlic powder
    1 teaspoon Italian seasoning
    1 jar (26 ounces) spaghetti sauce
    2 cups (8 ounces) shredded mozzarella cheese

1. Preheat oven to 350°F. Combine bread crumbs and Parmesan cheese in shallow bowl. Place chicken breast halves one at a time in bread crumb mixture, pressing to coat both sides.

2. Heat margarine in large skillet over medium high heat. Cook chicken in batches until browned on both sides. Transfer chicken to a 13×9-inch casserole coated with nonstick cooking spray. Top with broccoli, sprinkle with garlic powder and Italian seasoning and cover with spaghetti sauce. Sprinkle evenly with cheese.

3. Bake 25 minutes or until hot and bubbly and chicken is no longer pink in center. *Makes 12 servings*

Chicken Veggie Casserole
Cynthia Chamberlin | Blythe, Georgia

    1 can (10¾ ounces) condensed cheese soup, undiluted
    1 cup milk
 1½ cups cooked chicken, cut into bite-size pieces
    1 can (about 15 ounces) mixed vegetables
    1 can (about 16 ounces) sliced potatoes
    2 cups biscuit mix
    2 tablespoons mayonnaise
    1 egg

1. Preheat oven to 400°F.

2. Bring soup and milk to a boil over medium-high heat in large saucepan, stirring constantly. Stir in chicken, vegetables and potatoes. Pour into 13×9-inch baking dish.

3. Combine biscuit mix, mayonnaise and egg in medium bowl; mix just until crumbly. Sprinkle over chicken mixture.

4. Bake, uncovered, 30 minutes or until browned and bubbly.

Makes 4 to 6 servings

Chicken Broccoli Rice Casserole

Shelley Hill | Milwaukie, Oregon

    3 cups cooked long grain rice
    4 boneless skinless chicken breasts (about 1 pound), cooked and cut
        into bite-size pieces
 1½ pounds broccoli, steamed until tender and cut into bite-size pieces
    2 cans (10¾ ounces each) condensed cream of celery soup,
        undiluted
  ¾ cup mayonnaise
  ½ cup whole milk
    2 teaspoons curry powder
    3 cups (12 ounces) shredded sharp Cheddar cheese

1. Preheat oven to 350°F.

2. Butter 13×9-inch baking dish. Place cooked rice evenly into dish. Arrange chicken and broccoli on top. Mix together soup, mayonnaise, milk and curry powder in medium bowl; pour over chicken and broccoli. Top with cheese.

3. Cover loosely with foil and bake 45 minutes or until cheese melts and casserole is heated through.

Makes 4 to 6 servings

TEX-MEX
FIESTA

Green Chile-Chicken Casserole
Lori Stokes | Odessa, Texas

 4 cups shredded cooked chicken
1½ cups green enchilada sauce
 1 can (10¾ ounces) condensed cream of chicken soup, undiluted
 1 container (8 ounces) sour cream
 1 can (4 ounces) diced green chilies
 ½ cup vegetable oil
 12 (6-inch) corn tortillas
1½ cups (6 ounces) Colby-Jack cheese, divided

1. Preheat oven to 325°F. Grease 13×9-inch baking dish.

2. Combine chicken, enchilada sauce, soup, sour cream and chilies in large skillet over medium-high heat. Stir until warm.

3. Heat oil in separate deep skillet . Fry tortillas just until soft, drain on paper towels. Place 4 tortillas on bottom of prepared casserole. Layer with ⅓ chicken mixture and ½ cup cheese. Repeat layers twice.

4. Bake 15 to 20 minutes or until cheese is melted and casserole is heated through. *Makes 6 servings*

Green Chile-Chicken Casserole

Zucornchile Rajas Bake

Elaine Sweet | Dallas, Texas

2 cups tomato sauce
2 tablespoons chili powder
2 tablespoons tomato paste
1 tablespoon cider vinegar
1 teaspoon ground cumin
½ teaspoon salt
½ teaspoon garlic powder
¼ teaspoon ground red pepper
   Vegetable oil for frying
6 corn tortillas
3 cups sliced zucchini
1½ cups (6 ounces) shredded Monterey Jack or manchego cheese, divided
1 cup corn kernels
1 can (4 ounces) diced green chiles, drained
½ to 1 cup sour cream
3 green onions, chopped

1. Preheat oven to 350°F. Oil 13×9-inch baking dish.

2. Combine tomato sauce, chili powder, tomato paste, vinegar, cumin, salt, garlic powder and red pepper in medium saucepan. Bring to a boil over high heat; reduce heat to low and simmer 10 minutes, stirring occasionally.

3. Meanwhile, slice tortillas into ¼-inch strips. Heat enough oil to cover bottom of medium skillet by ½ inch. Fry tortilla strips in batches until crisp; drain on paper towels.

4. Steam zucchini for 5 minutes; drain. Transfer to large bowl. Add ¾ cup cheese, corn, chilies, and tortilla strips. Toss lightly to combine; spoon into prepared baking dish. Spread tomato sauce mixture over zucchini mixture and top with remaining ¾ cup cheese. Bake 30 minutes or until heated through.

5. Spread sour cream over top and sprinkle with green onions. Serve immediately.
   Makes 6 to 8 servings

Zucornchile Rajas Bake

Taco Salad Casserole

Tammy Rose | Princeton, West Virginia

1 pound ground beef
1 cup chopped onion
1 can (15 ounces) chili with beans
1 can (14½ ounces) diced tomatoes, undrained
1 can (4 ounces) chopped green chilies, undrained
1 package (about 1 ounce) taco seasoning mix
1 bag (12 ounces) nacho-flavored tortilla chips, divided
2 cups (8 ounces) shredded Cheddar cheese
2 cups (8 ounces) shredded mozzarella cheese
3 to 4 cups shredded lettuce
1 jar (8 ounces) prepared taco sauce
½ cup sour cream

1. Preheat oven to 350°F.

2. Cook and stir beef and onion in large skillet over medium heat until meat is no longer pink; drain fat. Add chili with beans, tomatoes, green chilies and taco seasoning; cook and stir until heated through.

3. Crush nacho chips and place half in 2½-quart casserole. Pour meat mixture over chips and top with cheeses and remaining chips. Bake 30 to 40 minutes or until hot and bubbly.

4. Serve over bed of lettuce; top with taco sauce and sour cream.

Makes 6 to 8 servings

Beefy Texas Cheddar Bake

Peter Halferty | Corpus Christi, Texas

1½ pounds lean ground beef
1 cup chopped onion
2 cans (10¾ ounces each) condensed tomato soup, preferably
    Mexican-style, undiluted
2 cups beef broth
1 box (6 ounces) corn bread stuffing mix
4 tablespoons margarine or butter, melted
2 teaspoons ground cumin
2 teaspoons ground chili powder
2 cups (8 ounces) shredded Mexican cheese blend

1. Preheat oven to 350°F. Grease 3-quart casserole.

2. Cook and stir beef and onion in a large skillet over medium heat for 5 minutes or until meat is no longer pink; drain fat. Spoon into prepared casserole.

3. Mix soup, broth, stuffing mix, margarine, cumin and chili powder in large bowl until combined. Spoon evenly over beef mixture. Top with cheese.

4. Bake 30 minutes or until heated through.   *Makes 8 servings*

Home Cook's HINT

When buying ground beef it helps to know that USDA standards require all ground beef to be at least 70 percent lean. Ground sirloin and ground round are leaner. When looking for the best price, keep in mind that leaner cuts cost more per pound, but produce less fat to drain off after cooking.

Cheesy Chicken Enchiladas

Julie DeMatteo | Clementon, New Jersey

¼ cup (½ stick) butter or margarine
1 cup chopped onion
2 cloves garlic, minced
¼ cup all-purpose flour
1 cup chicken broth
4 ounces cream cheese, softened
2 cups (8 ounces) shredded Mexican cheese blend, divided
1 cup shredded cooked chicken
1 can (7 ounces) chopped green chilies, drained
½ cup diced pimientos
6 (8-inch) flour tortillas, warmed
¼ cup chopped fresh cilantro
¾ cup prepared salsa

1. Preheat oven to 350°F. Spray 13×9-inch baking dish with nonstick cooking spray.

2. Melt butter in medium saucepan over medium heat. Add onion and garlic; cook and stir until onion is tender. Add flour, cook and stir 1 minute. Gradually whisk in chicken broth; cook and stir 2 to 3 minutes or until slightly thickened. Add cream cheese; stir until melted. Stir in ½ cup cheese, chicken, chilies and pimientos.

3. Spoon about ⅓ cup mixture onto each tortilla. Roll up and place in prepared baking dish seam-side down. Pour remaining mixture evenly on top and sprinkle with remaining 1½ cups cheese.

4. Bake 20 minutes or until bubbly and lightly browned. Sprinkle with cilantro and serve with salsa. *Makes 6 servings*

Cheesy Chicken Enchiladas 93

Cha-Cha-Cha Casserole
Diane Halferty | Corpus Christi, Texas

1 can (about 7 ounces) whole green chilies, drained
1 pound ground turkey or chicken
1 cup chopped onion
1 tablespoon chili powder (or more to taste)
3 cloves garlic, minced
1 teaspoon ground cumin
1 teaspoon salt (optional)
1 can (10 ounces) diced tomatoes and green chilies, undrained
2 cups frozen corn, thawed, or 2 cups canned whole kernel corn, drained
1 can (16 ounces) refried beans
2 cups (8 ounces) shredded Mexican cheese blend
2 cups crushed tortilla chips
1 cup seeded, diced fresh tomato
½ cup sliced green onions

1. Preheat oven to 375°F. Cut chilies in half lengthwise and arrange in single layer in 8-inch square baking dish coated with nonstick cooking spray.

2. Spray medium nonstick skillet with nonstick cooking spray. Cook and stir turkey, onion, chili powder, garlic, cumin and salt, if desired, over medium heat, until turkey is no longer pink. Add canned tomatoes and cook about 10 minutes until liquid evaporates.

3. Add meat mixture to casserole; top with corn, then beans. Sprinkle with cheese and crushed chips. Bake for 30 minutes; let stand 5 minutes before serving. Garnish with fresh tomatoes and green onions. *Makes 6 servings*

Summer Fiesta Casserole

Barbara J. Johnson | Moses Lake, Washington

2 pounds ground beef
1 medium onion, chopped
1 package (about 1 ounce) taco seasoning mix
4 to 6 potatoes, peeled and cut into ½-inch cubes (about 4 cups)
1 to 2 tablespoons vegetable oil
4 cups sliced zucchini
1 can (14½ ounces) diced tomatoes with onion and garlic, undrained
1½ cups (6 ounces) shredded Mexican cheese blend

1. Preheat oven to 350°F. Spray 4-quart casserole with nonstick cooking spray.

2. Cook beef and onion in large skillet over medium heat until meat is no longer pink, stirring to separate meat; drain fat. Add taco seasoning and cook according to package directions. Transfer meat mixture to prepared casserole.

3. Add potatoes to same skillet; cook and stir over medium heat until potatoes are browned, adding oil as needed to prevent sticking. Add zucchini; cook and stir until beginning to soften. Transfer to casserole; top with tomatoes and cheese.

4. Bake 10 to 15 minutes or until cheese is melted and casserole is heated through. *Makes 4 to 6 servings*

Barbara says: Serve with tortilla chips, sour cream and salsa.

Taco Casserole

Etta Delores Faultry | Alvin, Texas

2 pounds ground beef
1 teaspoon salt
1 teaspoon garlic powder
1 teaspoon cumin
1 teaspoon ground red pepper
1 teaspoon crushed red pepper flakes
1 teaspoon paprika
1 teaspoon chili powder
1 bag (12 ounces) nacho-flavored tortilla chips, crushed
1 can (10 ounces) diced tomatoes and green chilies, undrained
½ cup chopped green onions
1 cup (4 ounces) shredded Mexican cheese blend
½ cup sour cream (optional)

1. Preheat oven to 375°F.

2. Combine beef, salt, garlic powder, cumin, ground red pepper, red pepper flakes, paprika and chili powder in large skillet. Cook and stir over medium-high heat until meat is no longer pink; drain fat.

3. Add chips and tomatoes; stir well. Transfer to 13×9-inch casserole.

4. Bake 30 to 40 minutes or until bubbly. Sprinkle with onions and cheese. Top with sour cream, if desired. *Makes 4 to 6 servings*

Picadillo Tamale Casserole

Julie DeMatteo | Clementon, New Jersey

1½ pounds lean ground beef
1 cup chopped onion
2 cans (about 10 ounces each) diced tomatoes with green chilies
½ cup chicken broth
½ teaspoon ground cinnamon
6 tablespoons slivered almonds
6 tablespoons raisins
2 rolls (1 pound each) prepared polenta, cut into ½-inch-thick slices
2 cups (8 ounces) shredded Mexican cheese blend

1. Preheat oven to 350°F.

2. Cook and stir beef and onion in large skillet over medium heat for 5 minutes or until meat is no longer pink; drain fat.

3. Add tomatoes, chicken broth and cinnamon; simmer 2 to 3 minutes. Stir in almonds and raisins.

4. Layer ½ of polenta slices, ½ of meat mixture and ½ of cheese in 13×9-inch casserole. Repeat layers.

5. Bake 25 to 30 minutes or until hot and bubbly.

Makes 8 servings

Home Cook's HINT

What's Italian polenta doing in a Tex-Mex recipe? Polenta is simply the Italian name for cornmeal mush. Of course, cornmeal is a major ingredient in much of Mexican cooking from tamales to cornbread. Using prepared polenta is a clever shortcut that eliminates the extra work of preparing a cornmeal dough from scratch.

Picadillo Tamale Casserole

Turkey-Tortilla Bake

9 (6-inch) corn tortillas
½ pound 93% fat-free ground turkey
½ cup chopped onion
¾ cup mild or medium taco sauce
1 can (4 ounces) chopped green chilies, drained
½ cup frozen corn, thawed
½ cup (2 ounces) shredded reduced-fat Cheddar cheese
Sour cream (optional)

1. Preheat oven to 400°F. Place tortillas on large baking sheet, overlapping tortillas as little as possible. Bake 4 minutes; turn tortillas. Continue baking 2 minutes or until crisp. Cool completely on wire rack.

2. Heat medium nonstick skillet over medium heat until hot. Add turkey and onion. Cook and stir 5 minutes or until turkey is no longer pink and onion is tender. Add taco sauce, chilies and corn. Reduce heat and simmer 5 minutes.

3. Break 3 tortillas and arrange over bottom of 1½-quart casserole. Spoon half the turkey mixture over tortillas; sprinkle with half the cheese. Repeat layers. Bake 10 minutes or until cheese is melted and casserole is heated through. Break remaining tortillas and sprinkle over casserole. Garnish with sour cream, if desired.   *Makes 4 servings*

Esperanza's Enchiladas

Linda S. Killion Scott | Santa Rosa, California

  1 cup vegetable oil
 12 corn tortillas, cut into 1-inch pieces
1½ to 2 pounds ground beef
  ⅓ cup finely chopped yellow onion
  1 can (10½ ounces) enchilada sauce
  1 can (8 ounces) tomato sauce
  ¼ cup water
  1 envelope (about 1 ounce) taco or enchilada seasoning mix
  2 cups (8 ounces) shredded mild Cheddar cheese
  2 cups (8 ounces) shredded Monterey Jack cheese
  1 can (6 ounces) black olives, drained and chopped
  6 green onions, finely chopped
    Sour cream (optional)
    Guacamole (optional)

1. Preheat oven to 350°F.

2. Heat oil in medium skillet over medium-high heat. Add enough tortilla pieces to fill, but not crowd the skillet; fry until crisp. Remove with slotted spoon; set aside to drain on paper towels. Repeat with remaining tortilla pieces.

3. Cook and stir ground beef and onion in large skillet over medium-high heat stirring to break up meat until beef is browned; drain fat. Add enchilada sauce, tomato sauce, water and taco seasoning mix. Bring to a boil over high heat. Reduce heat to low and simmer 20 minutes.

4. Combine beef mixture with ⅔ of fried tortilla pieces in large bowl; transfer to 13×9-inch baking dish. Top with remaining ⅓ of tortilla pieces, cheeses, olives and green onions. Bake until cheeses are melted, about 5 to 10 minutes. Garnish with sour cream and guacamole, if desired. *Makes 6 to 8 servings*

Esperanza's Enchiladas 103

Mexican Lasagna

Kay Butram | Aurora, Ohio

  1 pound ground beef
  1 envelope (about 1 ounce) taco seasoning
  1 can (14½ ounces) Mexican-style diced tomatoes
1½ teaspoons chili powder
  1 teaspoon ground cumin
  ½ teaspoon salt
  ½ teaspoon crushed red pepper
  2 cups (16 ounces) sour cream
  1 can (4 ounces) diced chilies, drained
  6 green onions, chopped
  6 to 7 (8-inch) flour tortillas
  1 can (15 ounces) corn, drained
  2 cups (8 ounces) shredded Cheddar cheese

1. Preheat oven to 350°F. Grease 13×9-inch baking dish.

2. Cook and stir ground beef with taco seasoning in large skillet over medium heat until meat is no longer pink. Drain fat; set aside.

3. Mix tomatoes, chili powder, cumin, salt and red pepper in medium bowl. Set aside.

3. Combine sour cream, chilies and green onions in separate small bowl.

4. Layer ⅓ of tomato mixture, 2 tortillas, ⅓ of sour cream mixture, ⅓ of meat mixture, ⅓ of corn and ⅓ of cheese in prepared casserole. Repeat layers twice.

5. Bake 35 minutes or until bubbly. Let stand 15 minutes before serving. Garnish with olives and additional green onions, if desired.

Makes 4 servings

Chicken Chile Relleno Casserole

Julie De Matteo | Clementon, New Jersey

    3 cups diced cooked chicken
    1 can (about 7 ounces) chopped green chiles
1½ cups shredded Pepper-Jack or Mexican cheese blend, divided
1½ cups salsa, divided
    ¾ cup milk
    3 eggs
    ¼ cup flour
    1 teaspoon chili powder
    2 tablespoons minced fresh cilantro

1. Preheat oven to 350°F. Spray 2-quart casserole with nonstick cooking spray.

2. Spread chicken in casserole, top with chiles and ¾ cup cheese. Whisk together ½ cup salsa, milk, eggs, flour and chili powder in medium bowl. Stir in ¼ cup cheese; pour over chicken.

3. Sprinkle with remaining ½ cup cheese. Bake 25 to 30 minutes until set and cheese is lightly browned. Sprinkle with cilantro and serve with remaining 1 cup salsa. *Makes 6 servings*

Home Cook's HINT

Now that good selection of prepared salsas is readily available almost everywhere, don't limit their use to Mexican foods. Salsa tastes great on grilled meats or fish and is a zesty topping for baked potatoes, too. Try stirring salsa into a chopped salad or cooked vegetables. And for a quick dip, just add a few tablespoons of your favorite salsa to sour cream or yogurt.

Easy Chicken Chalupas

    1 roasted chicken (about 2 pounds)
    12 flour tortillas
    2 cups reduced-fat shredded Cheddar cheese
    1 cup mild green salsa
    1 cup mild red salsa

1. Preheat oven to 350°F. Spray 13×9-inch baking dish with cooking spray.

2. Remove chicken meat from bones and shred. Discard bones and skin.

3. Lay 1 or 2 tortillas in bottom of prepared dish, overlapping slightly. Layer tortillas with chicken, cheese and salsas. Repeat layers until baking dish is full. Finish with cheese and salsas.

4. Bake casserole 25 minutes or until bubbly and hot.

Makes 6 servings

Home Cook's HINT

Serve this easy main dish with some custom toppings on the side. Offer reduced-fat sour cream, chopped cilantro, sliced black olives (pre-sliced from a can, of course!), sliced green onions (from the salad bar) and sliced avocado.

Easy Chicken Chalupas 107

Mexican Rice Olé

Kathy Schmalz | Westerville, Ohio

1 teaspoon vegetable oil
1 cup uncooked long-grain rice
1 clove garlic, minced
1 teaspoon salt
1 can (about 14 ounces) chicken broth
1 can (10¾ ounces) condensed cream of onion soup, undiluted
¾ cup reduced-fat sour cream
1 can (4 ounces) chopped green chilies, undrained
⅓ cup prepared salsa
1 teaspoon ground cumin
1 cup (4 ounces) shredded Cheddar cheese
1 can (about 2 ounces) sliced black olives, drained

1. Preheat oven to 350°F. Coat 3-quart casserole with nonstick cooking spray.

2. Heat oil in large skillet over medium heat. Cook and stir rice, salt and garlic 2 or 3 minutes until rice is well coated. Add enough water to broth to equal 2 cups. Pour into skillet and simmer, stirring occasionally, about 15 minutes or until rice is tender.

3. Remove skillet from heat and add onion soup, sour cream, chilies, salsa and cumin; mix well. Spoon into prepared casserole; bake 20 minutes.

4. Top with cheese and olives. Bake additional 5 to 10 minutes until cheese melts and casserole is heated through.   *Makes 4 servings*

Kathy says: Cooked, chopped chicken may be added to make this casserole a one-dish meal.

Chilaquiles

1 can (10¾ ounces) condensed cream of chicken soup, undiluted
½ cup mild green salsa
1 can (4 ounces) diced green chilies, undrained
8 cups tortilla chips
2 to 3 cups shredded cooked chicken or turkey
2 cups (8 ounces) shredded Cheddar cheese
  Sliced pitted black olives for garnish
  Cilantro sprigs for garnish

Preheat oven to 350°F. Combine soup and salsa in medium bowl; stir in green chilies. Place ⅓ of chips in 2- to 2½-quart casserole; top with ⅓ of chicken. Spread ⅓ of soup mixture over chicken; sprinkle with ⅓ of cheese. Repeat layering. Bake, uncovered, 15 minutes or until casserole is heated through and cheese is melted. Garnish with olives and cilantro. *Makes 6 servings*

Casser-Olé

Julie DeMatteo | Clementon, New Jersey

1 pound lean ground beef
2 cups salsa
1½ cups water
1 can (about 15 ounces) black beans, rinsed and drained
1 cup corn
1 cup uncooked long-grain rice
2 cups (8 ounces) shredded Pepper-Jack cheese

1. Preheat oven to 350°F. Cook and stir ground beef in a large ovenproof skillet or Dutch oven over medium heat until no longer pink, stirring to separate meat. Drain fat.

2. Add salsa, water, beans and corn; bring to a boil. Stir in rice, cover and bake 50 to 60 minutes or until rice is tender and liquid is absorbed.

3. Sprinkle with cheese and return to oven for 5 minutes or until cheese melts. *Makes 6 to 8 servings*

Mexican Omelet Roll-Ups
with Avocado Sauce

8 eggs
2 tablespoons milk
1 tablespoon margarine or butter
1½ cups (6 ounces) shredded Monterey Jack cheese
1 large tomato, seeded and chopped
¼ cup chopped fresh cilantro
8 (7-inch) corn tortillas
1½ cups salsa
2 medium avocados, chopped
¼ cup reduced-fat sour cream
2 tablespoons diced green chiles
1 tablespoon fresh lemon juice
1 teaspoon hot pepper sauce
¼ teaspoon salt

1. Preheat oven to 350°F. Spray 13×9-inch baking dish with nonstick cooking spray.

2. Whisk eggs and milk in medium bowl until blended. Melt margarine in large skillet over medium heat; add egg mixture to skillet. Cook and stir 5 minutes or until eggs are set, but still soft. Remove from heat. Stir in cheese, tomato and cilantro.

3. Spoon about ⅓ cup egg mixture evenly down center of each tortilla. Roll up tortillas and place seam side down in prepared dish. Pour salsa evenly over tortillas.

4. Cover tightly with foil and bake 20 minutes or until heated through.

5. Meanwhile, process avocados, sour cream, chiles, lemon juice, hot pepper sauce and salt in food processor or blender until smooth. Serve with avocado sauce. *Makes 8 servings*

Mexican Omelet Roll-Up with Avocado Sauce   111

VERY
VEGGIE

Mediterranean Vegetable Bake
Marilyn Pocius | Oak Park, Illinois

2 tomatoes, sliced
1 small red onion, sliced
1 medium zucchini, sliced
1 small eggplant, sliced
1 large portobella mushroom cap, sliced
2 cloves garlic, finely chopped
3 tablespoons olive oil
2 teaspoons chopped fresh rosemary
⅔ cup white wine
Salt and pepper

1. Preheat oven to 350°F. Oil bottom of 13×9-inch baking pan or 10-inch pie pan.

2. Arrange slices of vegetables in rows, alternating different types and overlapping slices in pan to make an attractive arrangement. Sprinkle garlic evenly over top. Mix olive oil with rosemary in small bowl; spread over top.

3. Pour wine over vegetables, season with salt and pepper and loosely cover with foil. Bake 20 minutes. Uncover and bake an additional 10 to 15 minutes or until vegetables are soft.   *Makes 4 servings*

Marilyn says: Serve this with crusty bread to sop up the delicious juices. Feel free to use whatever vegetables you have on hand or in your garden.

Fruited Corn Pudding
Carole Resnick | Cleveland, Ohio

5 cups frozen corn, thawed and divided
5 eggs
½ cup milk
1½ cups heavy cream
⅓ cup unsalted butter, melted and cooled
1 teaspoon vanilla
½ teaspoon salt
¼ teaspoon ground nutmeg
3 tablespoons dried cranberries or raisins
3 tablespoons finely chopped dates
3 tablespoons finely chopped dried apricots
2 tablespoons finely chopped dried pears, or other dried fruit

1. Preheat oven to 350°F. Butter a 13×9-inch baking dish; set aside.

2. In food processor, combine 3½ cups corn, eggs, and milk; process until mixture is almost smooth.

3. Transfer corn mixture to large bowl. Add cream, butter, vanilla, salt and nutmeg; stir until well combined. Add remaining 1½ cups corn, cranberries, dates, apricots and pears. Stir well. Pour mixture into prepared baking dish.

4. Bake until custard is set and top begins to brown, about 50 to 60 minutes. Remove from oven and allow to sit for 10 to 15 minutes before serving. *Makes 8 to 10 servings*

Home Cook's HINT

To make chopping dried fruit easier, spray the knife or food processor blade with nonstick cooking spray before beginning. Placing the fruit in the freezer an hour ahead of time aids chopping, too. Some dried fruits, like apricots, are easier to snip with a kitchen shears than chop with a knife.

Southwest Spaghetti Squash

Lynda McCormick | Burkburnett, Texas

1 spaghetti squash (about 3 pounds)
1 can (about 14 ounces) Mexican-style diced tomatoes, undrained
1 can (about 14 ounces) black beans, rinsed and drained
¾ cup (3 ounces) shredded Monterey Jack cheese, divided
¼ cup finely chopped cilantro
1 teaspoon ground cumin
¼ teaspoon garlic salt
¼ teaspoon freshly ground black pepper

1. Preheat oven to 350°F. Cut squash in half lengthwise. Remove and discard seeds. Place squash, cut side down, on greased baking pan. Bake 45 minutes to 1 hour or until just tender. Using fork, remove spaghetti-like strands from hot squash and place strands in large bowl. (Use oven mitts to protect hands.)

2. Add tomatoes, beans, ½ cup cheese, cilantro, cumin, garlic salt and pepper to squash and stir well.

3. Spray 1½-quart casserole with nonstick cooking spray. Spoon mixture into casserole. Sprinkle with remaining ¼ cup cheese.

4. Bake, uncovered, 30 to 35 minutes or until heated through. Serve immediately. *Makes 4 servings*

Lynda says: This is a very simple dish you can throw together in a few minutes, then bake. Great for those nights you want to go meatless! Also a "kid-friendly" meal.

Carrie's Sweet Potato Casserole

Carrie Anderson | Hyattsville, Maryland

6 cups (about 3 pounds) cooked and peeled sweet potatoes
½ cup (1 stick) butter, softened
1 teaspoon vanilla
½ cup sugar
2 eggs, beaten
½ cup evaporated milk
  Topping (recipe follows)
1 cup pecans, chopped

1. Prepare topping; set aside. Preheat oven to 350°F. Grease 13×9-inch baking dish.

2. Mash sweet potatoes with butter in large bowl. Beat with electric mixer until light and fluffy.

3. One at a time, add vanilla, sugar, eggs and evaporated milk, beating after each addition. Pour into prepared baking dish. Spoon on topping and sprinkle with pecans.

4. Bake 25 minutes until heated through.   *Makes 8 to 12 servings*

Topping: Combine 1 cup packed brown sugar, ½ cup all-purpose flour and ⅓ cup melted butter in medium bowl.

Home Cook's HINT

This casserole also works well and looks pretty in individual-size serving dishes. Grease 8 (6-ounce) ovenproof ramekins and fill almost to the top with the sweet potato mixture. Top as in the recipe above and bake 20 minutes at 350°F or until heated through.

Zucchini-Carrot Casserole

Sharon Morris | Neoga, Illinois

½ cup (1 stick) margarine, melted
1 package (about 6 ounces) herb-flavored stuffing mix
2 cups fresh cubed zucchini, blanched and drained
1 can (14 ounces) condensed cream of celery soup, undiluted
1 cup grated carrots
1 small onion, chopped
½ cup sour cream
½ cup shredded Cheddar cheese

1. Preheat oven to 350°F.

1. Combine melted margarine and dry stuffing mix in medium bowl; set aside 1 cup for topping. place remaining stuffing in 13×9-inch baking dish.

2. Mix zucchini, soup, carrots, onion, and sour cream. Pour mixture over stuffing in baking dish. Top with reserved stuffing mix and cheese. Bake 40 to 45 minutes or until heated through and cheese is melted.

Makes 8 servings

Broccoli Casserole

Bobbie Gordon | Highland Park, Illinois

2 packages (10 ounces each) chopped frozen broccoli
1 container (16 ounces) cottage cheese
1½ cups (6 ounces) grated Cheddar cheese
4 eggs, lightly beaten
6 tablespoons (¾ stick) butter, melted
Salt and pepper

1. Preheat oven to 350°F.

2. Cook broccoli according to package directions; drain well. Mix broccoli and remaining ingredients in large bowl. Transfer to 2-quart casserole.

3. Bake 40 minutes until eggs are set and casserole is heated through.

Makes 6 to 8 servings

Eggplant Casserole

Vivian Woods | Tulsa, Oklahoma

1 eggplant, peeled and cut into ¼-inch slices
¾ cup seasoned croutons, crushed
¾ cup chopped red onion
1 can (6 ounces) tomato sauce
6 ounces sliced mozzarella cheese

1. Preheat oven to 350°F. Coat 8-inch square casserole with nonstick cooking spray. Boil eggplant in salted water to cover until tender. Drain, reserving ½-cup of boiling liquid.

2. Cover bottom of prepared casserole with eggplant slices, overlapping as necessary. Top with crushed croutons. Pour reserved liquid over croutons, then add onion. Spread tomato sauce over onion; top with cheese.

3. Bake 20 to 30 minutes or until hot and bubbly.

Makes 6 servings

Lisa's Corn Casserole

Lisa Garretson | Clinton, New Jersey

3 eggs, beaten
2 cans (about 15 ounces each) cream-style corn
1 can (15 ounces) whole kernel corn, drained
½ cup sugar
½ cup (1 stick) butter, melted
¾ cup milk
1 to 2 tablespoons flour

1. Preheat oven to 350°F. Grease 2-quart casserole.

2. Mix together eggs, cream-style and whole kernel corn, sugar and butter. In cup, stir milk into flour until smooth. Add milk mixture to corn mixture; blend well.

3. Pour into prepared casserole and bake 40 to 50 minutes or until set.

Makes 6 servings

Summer Squash Casserole

Darleen Presnell | Deep Gap, North Carolina

2 cups sliced yellow summer squash
1 medium carrot, thinly sliced
½ cup chopped onion
½ cup diced red or green bell pepper
½ teaspoon salt
⅛ teaspoon pepper
1 container (8 ounces) sour cream
1 can (10¾ ounces) condensed cream of chicken or mushroom
    soup, undiluted
1 cup (4 ounces) shredded Italian cheese blend
1 cup (4 ounces) shredded Cheddar cheese
1 package (6 ounces) stuffing mix

1. Preheat oven to 350°F. Combine squash, carrot, onion, bell pepper, salt and pepper in a medium saucepan; cover with water. Bring to a boil and cook 5 minutes or until tender; drain.

2. Combine sour cream and soup in 13×9-inch casserole; mix well. Stir in vegetable mixture and spread evenly. Sprinkle cheeses on top.

3. Top with dry stuffing mix. Bake, covered, 30 minutes or until heated through.   *Makes 6 servings*

Home Cook's HINT

Yellow summer squash (one variety is crookneck) is traditional in this southern casserole dish, but zucchini or even pattypan squash may be substituted. Choose small, firm squash with a bright color. There's no need to peel tender summer squash, just wash and slice it. One pound of squash yields about 3 cups sliced.

Eggplant Parmigiana

Theresa Moreau | Utica, New York

    2 eggs, beaten
 ¼ cup milk
    Dash of garlic powder
    Dash of onion powder
    Dash of salt
    Dash of pepper
    1 large eggplant, cut into ½-inch thick slices
 ½ cup seasoned bread crumbs
    Vegetable oil for frying
    1 jar (about 26 ounces) prepared pasta sauce
    4 cups (16 ounces) shredded mozzarella
 2½ cups (10 ounces) shredded Swiss cheese
 ¼ cup grated Parmesan cheese
 ¼ cup grated Romano cheese

1. Preheat oven to 350°F. Combine eggs, milk, garlic powder, onion powder, salt and pepper in shallow bowl. Dip eggplant in egg mixture and then coat in bread crumbs.

2. Add enough oil to large skillet to cover bottom by ¼-inch. Heat over medium-high heat. Brown eggplant in batches on both sides; drain on paper towels. Cover bottom of 13×9-inch baking dish with 2 or 3 tablespoons sauce. Layer ½ of eggplant, ½ of Swiss cheese, ½ of mozzarella and ½ of remaining sauce in dish. Repeat layers. Sprinkle with Parmesan and Romano cheeses.

3. Bake 30 minutes or until heated through and cheese is melted.

Makes 4 servings

Curried Cauliflower & Cashews

Marilyn Pocius | Oak Park, Illinois

1 medium head cauliflower, cut into florets (about 4 cups)
½ cup water
¾ cup unsalted toasted cashews, plus additional for garnish
3 tablespoons butter, divided
2 tablespoons all purpose flour
1 tablespoon curry powder
1¼ cups milk
 Salt and pepper
1 cup dry bread crumbs
1 jar prepared mango chutney (optional)

1. Preheat oven to 350°F. Butter a 2-quart casserole.

2. Place cauliflower in large, microwave safe dish. Add ½ cup water. Microwave at HIGH about 4 minutes or until almost tender. Drain and place in prepared casserole. Add cashews and stir to combine.

3. Melt 2 tablespoons butter in medium saucepan. Add flour and curry powder. Cook and stir over medium-high heat 2 minutes to form a paste. Add milk, whisking constantly; cook and stir until mixture thickens slightly. Season with salt and pepper.

4. Pour sauce over cauliflower mixture and stir to coat evenly. Top with bread crumbs and dot with remaining 1 tablespoon butter.

5. Bake 45 minutes or until lightly browned. Garnish with additional cashews and serve with chutney, if desired.

Marilyn says: Curry powders vary dramatically in terms of spiciness and flavor. Choose one that suits your taste and make sure it's fresh since curry powder loses much of its flavor quickly.

Curried Cauliflower & Cashews   127

Vegetable Casserole

Adele Simoni | Whiting, New Jersey

8 potatoes, peeled and cooked until tender
1 cup milk
¾ cup (1½ sticks) unsalted butter, divided
1 package (about 16 ounces) frozen spinach, cooked
    Salt and pepper
1 pound carrots, sliced, cooked until tender
1 pound green beans, cut into 1-inch pieces and cooked until tender
½ teaspoon paprika

1. Preheat oven to 375°F. Grease a 4-quart casserole or roasting pan.

2. Mash potatoes with milk and ½ cup butter until creamy. Set aside.

3. Spread spinach in prepared casserole and dot with 1 tablespoon butter; season with salt and pepper.

4. Layer ½ of potatoes over spinach, followed by carrots and string beans. Dot with another 1 tablespoon butter; season with salt and pepper.

5. Layer remaining ½ of potatoes on top. Dot with remaining 2 tablespoons butter and sprinkle with paprika. Bake 1 hour until heated through and lightly browned.   *Makes 10 to 12 servings*

Zucchini with Feta Casserole

June Holmes | Alpharetta, Georgia

4 medium zucchini, peeled
2 teaspoons butter or margarine
½ cup grated Parmesan cheese
⅓ cup crumbled feta cheese
2 eggs, beaten
2 tablespoons chopped fresh parsley
2 teaspoons chopped fresh marjoram
1 tablespoon flour
   Dash hot pepper sauce
   Salt
   Pepper

1. Preheat oven to 375°F. Grease 2-quart casserole.

2. Grate zucchini; drain in colander. Melt butter in medium skillet over medium heat. Add zucchini; cook and stir until slightly browned. Remove from heat.

3. Add remaining ingredients to skillet; mix well.

4. Pour into prepared casserole and bake 35 minutes until bubbly.

Makes 4 servings

Wild Rice Casserole

Philip A. Pinchotti | Freedom, Pennsylvania

1 cup wild rice, soaked overnight
1 large onion, chopped
1 cup (4 ounces) shredded Cheddar cheese
1 cup chopped mushrooms
1 cup chopped black olives
1 cup drained chopped canned tomatoes
1 cup tomato juice
⅓ cup vegetable oil
   Salt and pepper

1. Preheat oven to 350°F.

2. Drain rice. Combine rice and remaining ingredients except salt and pepper in large bowl.

3. Season with salt and pepper. Transfer to 1½-quart casserole. Cover and bake 1½ hours, or until rice is tender. *Makes 6 servings*

Philip says: This tastes even better reheated the next day.

Two Squash Risotto in a Bag

June Holmes | Alpharetta, Georgia

1 tablespoon flour
1 can (14½ ounces) plus 1 cup chicken broth
1 cup arborio rice
1 large onion, chopped
1 cup matchstick-size zucchini strips
1 cup matchstick-size yellow squash strips
½ cup (2 ounces) shredded mozzarella cheese
½ cup butter or margarine, melted
2 tablespoons balsamic vinegar
2 cloves garlic, minced
Bacon, crisp-cooked and crumbled (optional)

1. Preheat oven to 350°F.

2. Add flour to large oven-roasting bag and shake well. Combine all remaining ingredients, except bacon, in large bowl, mix well.

3. Pour into oven-roasting bag; close tightly and cut six ½-inch long slits in top of bag to allow steam to escape.

4. Place bag in 3-quart baking dish.

5. Bake 1 hour or until rice is tender and liquid is absorbed. Garnish with crumbled bacon, if desired. *Makes 4 to 6 servings*

Baked Risotto with Asparagus, Spinach & Parmesan

June Holmes | Alpharetta, Georgia

1 cup finely chopped onion
1 tablespoon olive oil
1 cup arborio (risotto) rice
8 cups (8 to 10 ounces) spinach leaves, torn into pieces
2 cups chicken broth
¼ teaspoon salt
¼ teaspoon ground nutmeg
½ cup Parmesan cheese, divided
1½ cups diagonally sliced asparagus

1. Preheat oven to 400°F. Spray 13×9-inch baking dish with nonstick cooking spray.

2. In large skillet heat olive oil over medium-high heat; add onion cook and stir 4 minutes or until tender. Add rice and stir well.

3. Stir in spinach, a handful at a time adding more as it wilts. Add broth, salt and nutmeg. Reduce heat and simmer 7 minutes. Stir in ¼ cup cheese.

5. Transfer to prepared baking dish. Cover tightly and bake 15 minutes.

6. Remove from oven and stir in asparagus; sprinkle with remaining ¼ cup cheese. Cover and bake 15 minutes more or until liquid is absorbed. *Makes 6 servings*

Home Cook's HINT

Classic Italian risotto requires a special short-grain, high-starch rice. Arborio is the most readily available. Never rinse arborio rice before cooking since you don't want to wash off the starchy coating that makes the finished dish creamy.

Baked Risotto with Asparagus, Spinach & Parmesan   133

Potatoes au Gratin

1½ pounds small red potatoes
6 tablespoons (¾ stick) butter, divided
3 tablespoons all-purpose flour
½ teaspoon salt
¼ teaspoon white pepper
1½ cups milk
1 cup (4 ounces) shredded Cheddar cheese
4 green onions, thinly sliced
¾ cup cracker crumbs

1. Preheat oven to 350°F. Spray 1-quart round casserole with nonstick cooking spray.

2. Place potatoes in 2-quart saucepan; add enough water to cover potatoes. Bring to a boil over high heat. Cook, uncovered, about 10 minutes or until partially done. Potatoes should still be firm in center. Drain and rinse in cold water until potatoes are cool. Drain and set aside.

3. Meanwhile, melt 4 tablespoons butter in medium saucepan over medium heat. Add flour, salt and pepper, stirring until smooth. Gradually add milk, stirring constantly until sauce is thickened. Add cheese, stirring until melted.

4. Cut potatoes crosswise into ¼-inch-thick slices. Layer ⅓ of potatoes in prepared dish. Top with ⅓ of onions and ⅓ of cheese sauce. Repeat layers twice, ending with cheese sauce.

5. Melt remaining 2 tablespoons butter. Combine cracker crumbs and butter in small bowl. Sprinkle evenly over top of casserole. Bake, uncovered, 35 to 40 minutes or until hot and bubbly and potatoes are tender. *Makes 4 to 6 servings*

Vegetable & Tofu Gratin

1 teaspoon olive oil
¾ cup thinly sliced fennel bulb
¾ cup thinly sliced onion
2 cloves garlic, minced
¾ cup cooked brown rice
2 tablespoons balsamic or red wine vinegar, divided
2 teaspoons dried Italian seasoning, divided
3 ounces firm tofu, crumbled
¼ cup crumbled feta cheese
2 to 3 ripe plum tomatoes, sliced ¼ inch thick
1 medium zucchini, sliced ¼ inch thick
⅛ teaspoon salt
⅛ teaspoon black pepper
¼ cup fresh bread crumbs
2 tablespoons freshly grated Parmesan cheese

1. Preheat oven to 400°F. Spray 1-quart shallow baking dish with nonstick cooking spray.

2. Heat oil in medium skillet over medium heat. Add fennel and onion. Cook about 10 minutes or until tender and lightly browned, stirring frequently. Add garlic; cook and stir 1 minute. Spread over bottom of prepared baking dish.

3. Combine rice, 1 tablespoon vinegar and ½ teaspoon Italian seasoning in small bowl. Spread over onion mixture.

4. Combine tofu, feta cheese, remaining 1 tablespoon vinegar and 1 teaspoon Italian seasoning in same small bowl; toss to combine. Spoon over rice.

5. Top with alternating rows of tomato and zucchini slices. Sprinkle with salt and pepper.

6. Combine bread crumbs, Parmesan cheese and remaining ½ teaspoon Italian seasoning in small bowl. Sprinkle over top. Spray bread crumb topping lightly with nonstick cooking spray. Bake 30 minutes or until heated through and topping is browned.

Makes 2 servings

Fresh Vegetable Casserole

8 small new potatoes
8 baby carrots
1 small cauliflower, broken into florets
4 stalks asparagus, cut into 1-inch pieces
3 tablespoons butter or margarine
3 tablespoons all-purpose flour
2 cups milk
  Salt
  Black pepper
¾ cup (3 ounces) shredded Cheddar cheese
  Chopped fresh cilantro

1. Steam vegetables until crisp-tender. Arrange vegetables in buttered 2-quart casserole. Preheat oven to 350°F.

2. To make sauce, melt butter in medium saucepan over medium heat. Stir in flour until smooth. Gradually stir in milk. Cook until thickened, stirring constantly. Season to taste with salt and pepper. Add cheese, stirring until cheese is melted. Pour sauce over vegetables and sprinkle with cilantro. Bake 15 minutes or until heated through.

Makes 4 to 6 servings

Sesame-Honey Vegetable Casserole

1 package (16 ounces) frozen mixed vegetable medley, such as baby
   carrots, broccoli, onions and red peppers, thawed and drained
3 tablespoons honey
1 tablespoon dark sesame oil
1 tablespoon soy sauce
2 teaspoons sesame seeds

1. Preheat oven to 350°F. Place vegetables in shallow, 1½-quart casserole dish or quiche pan.

2. Combine remaining ingredients; mix well. Drizzle evenly over vegetables. Bake 20 to 25 minutes or until vegetables are hot, stirring after 15 minutes.

Makes 4 to 6 servings

Fresh Vegetable Casserole   139

Spanish Rice & Squash

Charlotte Sue Taylor | Midway, West Virginia

2 small yellow summer squash, cut into ¼-inch slices
1 small zucchini, cut into ¼-inch slices
1 package (about 12 ounces) Spanish rice mix
2 cups water
1 can (about 14 ounces) diced tomatoes, undrained
1 can (about 4 ounces) sliced mushrooms, drained
3 tablespoons butter, melted
1 pound smoked sausage, cut into 4-inch pieces
1 can (about 3 ounces) French fried onions
1 cup shredded mozzarella cheese

1. Preheat oven to 350°F. Coat 3-quart casserole with nonstick cooking spray. Place sliced squash and zucchini in prepared casserole.

2. Combine rice mix, water, tomatoes, mushrooms, and butter in medium bowl, stir well. Pour over squash; top with sausage.

3. Cover and bake 20 minutes. Uncover and place onions around edge of casserole. Sprinkle cheese in center. Bake, uncovered, 5 to 10 minutes more or until cheese melts. *Makes 4 to 6 servings*

Polynesian Baked Beans

Lynda McCormick | Burkburnett, Texas

2 tablespoons olive oil
3 tablespoons chopped onion
2 cans (16 ounces each) baked beans
1 can (about 11 ounces) mandarin oranges, drained
1 can (about 8 ounces) pineapple chunks in juice, drained
½ cup chopped green bell pepper
1 can (about 4 ounces) deviled ham
¼ cup ketchup
2 tablespoons packed brown sugar
½ teaspoon salt (optional)
Dash hot pepper sauce

1. Preheat oven to 375°F. Heat oil in small skillet over medium heat. Add onion; cook and stir until transparent.

2. Combine onion and remaining ingredients in 2-quart casserole. Bake, uncovered, 30 to 35 minutes or until bubbly.

Makes 6 to 8 servings

Lynda says: This is a great recipe to double and can also be made in a slow cooker.

Spinach Casserole
Charlotte G Williams | St. Clair, Pennsylvania

2 packages (14 ounces each) frozen chopped spinach, thawed and
   squeezed dry
3 tablespoons butter
1 tablespoon flour
1 cup milk
2 eggs, separated
1 tablespoon chopped fresh parsley
   Salt and pepper
1 cup (4 ounces) shredded Cheddar cheese

1. Preheat oven to 350°F. Butter 2½ quart casserole.

2. Melt butter in medium saucepan over medium heat. Stir in flour and cook and stir 2 minutes. Gradually whisk in milk. Continue cooking until mixture thickens slightly. Gradually add egg yolks. Season with parsley, salt and pepper. Add cheese, stirring constantly until cheese melts. Transfer to medium bowl.

3. Add spinach to cheese sauce and stir until well combined; keep warm. Meanwhile, beat egg whites to stiff peaks in clean, dry bowl. Gently fold egg whites into spinach-cheese mixture.

4. Spoon into prepared casserole and bake 40 minutes or until center is set and looks dry. *Do not over bake.*

Makes 6 servings

CLASSIC
COMBINATIONS

Easy Vegetable Beef Stew
Jane Lindeman | Skokie, Illinois

1 pound beef for stew, cut into 1-inch pieces
1 can (14½ ounces) diced tomatoes
1 medium onion, cut into 8 wedges
4 carrots, cut into 1-inch pieces
1 green or red bell pepper, diced
1 rib celery, sliced
1 teaspoon Italian seasoning
½ teaspoon salt
½ teaspoon black pepper
1 tablespoon vegetable oil
1 package (8 ounces) sliced **mushrooms**

1. Combine beef pieces, tomatoes and onion in Dutch oven. Cover tightly; bake at 325°F 1 hour.

2. Add carrots, bell pepper, celery, Italian seasoning, salt and black pepper to beef mixture; stir. Cover; bake an additional 45 minutes or until beef and carrots are tender.

3. Heat oil in large skillet over medium heat. Add mushrooms; cook and stir 10 minutes or until lightly browned and tender. Stir mushrooms into beef stew. Adjust seasonings to taste.

Makes 4 servings

Variation: 2 unpeeled medium red potatoes, cut into 2-inch pieces, may be added with carrots.

Easy Vegetable Beef Stew

It's a Keeper Casserole

Carol A. Stone | Waverly, Tennessee

1 tablespoon vegetable oil
½ cup chopped onion
¼ cup chopped green pepper
1 clove garlic, minced
2 tablespoons all purpose flour
1 teaspoon sugar
½ teaspoon salt
½ teaspoon dried basil leaves
½ teaspoon pepper
1 can (about 16 ounces) tomatoes, cut up
1 package (about 16 ounces) frozen prepared meatballs, cooked
1½ cups cooked vegetables (any combination)
1 teaspoon beef bouillon granules
1 teaspoon Worcestershire sauce
1 can refrigerated buttermilk biscuits

1. Preheat oven to 400°F. Heat oil in large saucepan. Cook and stir onion, green pepper and garlic over medium heat until vegetables are tender.

2. Stir in flour, sugar, salt, basil and pepper. Slowly blend in tomatoes, meatballs, vegetables, bouillon and Worcestershire sauce. Cook and stir until slightly thicker and bubbling; pour into 2-quart casserole.

3. Unroll biscuits and place around the top of casserole and bake, uncovered, until biscuits are golden, about 15 minutes.

Makes 4 servings

Carol says: This casserole came together as an accident. I had forgotten I needed to bring a casserole to a church supper and had to use what I had on hand and quickly. I received so many requests for the recipe that I added it to my regulars. Use whatever you have on hand— hamburger, leftover beef or even sliced hot dogs.

Shrimp Creole

Marilyn Pocius | Oak Park, Illinois

2 tablespoons olive oil
1½ cups chopped green bell pepper
1 medium onion, chopped
⅔ cup chopped celery
2 cloves garlic, finely chopped
1 cup uncooked long grain rice
1 can (about 14 ounces) diced tomatoes, drained, juice reserved
½ teaspoon dried thyme leaves
1 teaspoon dried oregano leaves
¾ teaspoon salt
2 teaspoons hot sauce, or more to taste
   Freshly ground pepper
1 pound raw shrimp, peeled and deveined
1 tablespoon chopped fresh parsley (optional)

1. Preheat oven to 325°F. Heat olive oil in large skillet over medium-high heat. Add bell pepper, onion, celery and garlic; cook and stir 5 minutes or until vegetables soften.

2. Add rice to skillet; cook and stir five minutes over medium heat until rice is coated. Add tomatoes, thyme, oregano, salt, hot sauce and pepper to skillet; cook and stir to combine. Pour reserved juice into measuring cup. Add enough water to measuring cup to equal 1¾ cups liquid; add to skillet. Cook and stir 2 minutes to combine.

3. Transfer mixture to 2½-quart casserole. Stir in shrimp. Bake, covered, 55 minutes or until rice is tender and liquid is absorbed. Sprinkle with parsley, if desired. *Makes 4 to 6 servings*

My Mac & Cheese

Carrie A. Theroux | Saco, Maine

4 tablespoons (½ stick) butter
4 tablespoons flour
2 cups milk
½ pound sharp Cheddar cheese, cut into ½-inch cubes
8 slices (about 2 ounces) Pepper Jack cheese (optional)
½ cup chopped onion
2 cups (about 16 ounces) broccoli florets, steamed until tender
2 cups macaroni, cooked and drained
2 English muffins, chopped into ½-inch pieces

1. Preheat oven to 350°F.

2. Melt butter in large saucepan over medium heat. Stir in flour to make a smooth paste; cook and stir 2 minutes. Gradually add milk, stirring contantly until slightly thickened.

3. Add Cheddar cheese, pepper jack cheese, if desired, and onion to the milk sauce. Cook, stirring constantly, until cheese melts.

4. Add broccoli; stir well.

5. Place macaroni in 3-quart casserole. Add cheese and broccoli mixture; mix well. Sprinkle English muffin pieces evenly over top. Bake 15 to 20 minutes or until muffin pieces are golden brown.

Makes 4 to 6 servings

Home Cook's HINT

Broccoli can easily be steamed in your microwave. Place the florets in a microwavable dish. Add 1/4 cup of water. Cover; cook at HIGH 3 to 4 minutes or until crisp-tender.

Ham 'n' Apple Breakfast Casserole Slices

Diane Halferty | Corpus Christi, Texas

1 package (15 ounces) refrigerated pie crusts (2 crusts)
20 pieces (about 1 pound) thinly sliced ham, cut into bite-size pieces
1 can (21 ounces) apple pie filling
1 cup (4 ounces) shredded sharp Cheddar cheese
¼ cup plus 1 teaspoon sugar, divided
½ teaspoon ground cinnamon

1. Preheat oven to 425°F.

2. Place one crust in 9-inch pie pan, allowing edges to hang over sides. Arrange half the ham slices on bottom crust. Spoon apple filling onto ham. Arrange remaining ham on top of apples; cover with cheese.

3. Mix ¼ cup sugar and cinnamon in small bowl; sprinkle evenly over cheese. Arrange second crust over filling and crimp edges together. Brush crust lightly with water and sprinkle with remaining 1 teaspoon sugar. Cut slits for steam to escape.

4. Bake 20 to 25 minutes or until crust is golden-brown. Cool 15 minutes. Slice into wedges. *Makes 6 servings*

Diane says: This casserole can be assembled the night before, covered and refrigerated, then baked the next morning.

Ham 'n' Apple Breakfast Casserole Slices   151

Broccoli Chicken Cheese Fries Casserole

Maria L. Weiss | Somerset, Massachusetts

3 tablespoons vegetable oil
5 boneless chicken breasts (about 1½ pounds), cut into bite-size
    pieces
½ package (about 8 ounces) frozen potato nuggets
1 package (10 ounces) frozen broccoli florets, thawed
2 cans (10¾ ounces each) condensed cheese soup, undiluted
1 cup bread crumbs
2 tablespoons butter or margarine, melted

1. Preheat oven to 400°F. Grease 3½-quart casserole.

2. Heat oil in large skillet over medium-high heat; add chicken. Cook and stir 5 to 10 minutes until chicken is no longer pink; drain.

3. Meanwhile, bake potato nuggets on *ungreased* baking sheet for 10 minutes; remove from oven. *Reduce oven temperature to 350°F.*

4. Combine chicken, potato nuggets, broccoli and 1 can of cheese soup in large bowl. Pour mixture into prepared casserole and pour over remaining can of soup. Combine bread crumbs and melted butter in small bowl; sprinkle over top.

5. Bake at 350°F 20 minutes or until browned and bubbly.

Makes 6 to 8 servings

Chicken Noodle Casserole

Alicia Freed | Apple Valley, California

1 package (12 ounces) wide egg noodles
1 can (10¾ ounces) condensed cream of mushroom soup, undiluted
1 can (10¾ ounces) condensed cream of chicken soup, undiluted
1 can (6 ounces) cooked white chicken
½ cup milk
½ cup shredded Cheddar-Jack cheese
½ cup sour cream
1 cup dry bread crumbs

1. Prepare egg noodles as directed on package. Drain well then place in large saucepan.

2. Add soups, chicken, milk, cheese and sour cream.

3. Cook and stir over medium heat until heated through.

4. Pour into 13×9-inch casserole and top with bread crumbs.

5. Place casserole under broiler for 5 to 10 minutes or until crispy on top.

Make 4 to 6 servings

Easy Crab-Asparagus Pie

4 ounces crabmeat, flaked
1½ cups sliced asparagus, cooked
½ cup chopped onion, cooked
1 cup (4 ounces) shredded Monterey Jack cheese
¼ cup (1 ounce) grated Parmesan cheese
Black pepper
¾ cup all-purpose flour
¾ teaspoon baking powder
½ teaspoon salt
2 tablespoons butter or margarine, chilled
1½ cups milk
4 eggs, lightly beaten

1. Preheat oven to 350°F. Lightly grease 10-inch quiche dish or pie plate.

2. Layer crabmeat, asparagus and onion in prepared pie plate; top with cheeses. Season with pepper.

3. Combine flour, baking powder and salt in large bowl. With pastry blender or 2 knives, cut in butter until mixture forms coarse crumbs. Stir in milk and eggs; pour over vegetables and cheeses.

4. Bake 30 minutes or until filling is puffed and knife inserted near center comes out clean. Serve hot.

Makes 6 servings

Emily's Goulash

Emily Hale | Chicago, Illinois

½ cup all-purpose flour
3 teaspoons salt, divided
2 teaspoons pepper, divided
2 pounds beef chuck, cut into bite-size pieces
¼ cup plus 2 tablespoons vegetable oil, divided
2 shallots, finely chopped
3 cloves garlic, finely chopped
1 tablespoon paprika
1 large can (about 28 ounces) chopped tomatoes, undrained
3½ cups water
1 teaspoon dried parsley leaves
1 teaspoon dried thyme leaves
2 bay leaves
3 tablespoons sour cream

1. Mix flour, 2 teaspoons salt and 1 teaspoon pepper in shallow bowl. Heat large Dutch oven over high heat. Add ¼ cup vegetable oil. Dip pieces of beef into flour mixture, shake off excess and brown thoroughly in batches in Dutch oven. Do not crowd pan. Transfer beef to plate and set aside. Drain remaining oil and wipe out pan.

2. Preheat oven to 275°F. Add 2 tablespoons oil to Dutch oven; cook and stir shallots and garlic over medium heat about 2 minutes. Add tomatoes and paprika; simmer 2 minutes. Add reserved beef, any accumulated juices, water, parsley, thyme and bay leaves. Cover; bake about 1½ hours until beef is tender.

3. Remove from oven; simmer over medium heat, stirring occasionally, 20 minutes. Reduce heat to low and stir in sour cream; cook and stir until liquid has reduced to sauce-like consistency and beef is very tender, about 20 minutes. Stir in remaining 1 teaspoon salt and season with pepper. Remove and discard bay leaves. Serve over buttered egg noodles sprinkled with parsley, if desired.

Makes 4 to 6 servings

Cheesy Tuna Pie

Diane Nemitz | Ludington, Michigan

2 cups cooked rice
2 cans (6 ounces each) tuna, drained and flaked
1 cup mayonnaise
1 cup (4 ounces) shredded Cheddar cheese
½ cup sour cream
½ cup thinly sliced celery
1 can (4 ounces) sliced black olives
2 tablespoons onion flakes
1 unbaked pie crust

1. Preheat oven to 350°F. Spray 9-inch, deep-dish pie pan with nonstick cooking spray.

2. Combine all ingredients except pie crust in medium bowl; mix well. Spoon into prepared pie pan. Place pie crust over tuna mixture; press edges to pie pan to seal. Cut slits for steam to escape.

3. Bake 20 minutes or until crust is browned and filling is bubbly.

Makes 6 servings

Diane says: This is super easy! It uses ingredients I always have on hand, and I love the made-from-scratch flavor.

Biscuit-Topped Hearty Steak Pie

1½ pounds top round steak, cooked and cut into 1-inch cubes
1 package (9 ounces) frozen baby carrots
1 package (9 ounces) frozen peas and pearl onions
1 large baking potato, cooked and cut into ½-inch pieces
1 jar (18 ounces) home-style brown gravy
½ teaspoon dried thyme leaves
½ teaspoon black pepper
1 can (10 ounces) flaky buttermilk biscuits

1. Preheat oven to 375°F. Spray 2-quart casserole with nonstick cooking spray.

2. Combine steak, frozen vegetables and potato in prepared dish. Stir in gravy, thyme and pepper.

3. Bake, uncovered, 40 minutes. Remove from oven. *Increase oven temperature to 400°F.* Top with biscuits and bake 8 to 10 minutes or until biscuits are golden brown.   *Makes 6 servings*

Home Cook's HINT

This casserole can be prepared with leftovers of almost any kind. Other steaks, roast beef, stew meat, pork, lamb or chicken can be substituted for round steak; adjust the gravy flavor to complement the meat. Red potatoes can be used in place of a baking potato. Choose your favorite vegetable combination, such as broccoli, cauliflower and carrots or broccoli, corn and red peppers, as a substitute for the peas and carrots.

Biscuit-Topped Hearty Steak Pie   159

Delicious Ham & Cheese Puff Pie

Roxanne Chan | Albany, California

2 cups (about 1 pound) diced cooked ham
1 package (10 ounces) frozen chopped spinach, thawed and
 squeezed dry
½ cup diced red bell pepper
4 green onions, sliced
¾ cup all-purpose flour
¾ cup (3 ounces) shredded Swiss cheese
¾ cup milk
3 eggs
1 tablespoon prepared mustard
1 teaspoon grated lemon peel
1 teaspoon dried dill weed
½ teaspoon garlic salt
½ teaspoon ground black pepper
 Dill sprigs and lemon slices (optional)

1. Preheat oven to 425°F. Grease 2-quart casserole.

2. Combine ham, spinach, pepper and onions in prepared casserole.

3. Whisk together remaining ingredients in medium bowl; pour over ham mixture.

4. Bake 30 to 35 minutes or until puffed and browned. Cut into wedges and garnish with dill sprigs and lemon slices, if desired.

Makes 4 to 6 servings

Delicious Ham & Cheese Puff Pie

Four Cheese Mac & Cheese
Beth Shaw | Pawcatuck, Connecticut

1 package (16 ounces) macaroni, cooked and drained
4 cups milk
16 ounces sharp white Cheddar cheese, shredded
16 ounces American cheese, shredded
8 ounces Muenster cheese, shredded
8 ounces mozzarella cheese, shredded
½ cup bread crumbs

1. Preheat oven to 350°F. Heat milk to almost boiling in large saucepan over medium heat. *Reduce heat to low.* Gradually add cheeses, stirring constantly. Cook and stir about 5 minutes until all cheese has melted.

2. Place macaroni in 4-quart casserole. Pour cheese sauce over pasta and stir until well combined. Top with bread crumbs. Bake 1 hour or until browned and bubbly. *Makes 8 servings*

Honey-Baked Heaven
Yuki Mountjoy | Des Moines, Washington

8 large Granny Smith apples (or other tart apples), peeled and sliced
2 packages (8 ounces each) kielbasa sausage, cut into ½-inch slices
1⅓ cups honey
4 tablespoons water
1 tablespoon ground cinnamon
⅓ cup butter

1. Preheat oven to 350°F.

2. Butter 13×9-inch baking dish. Arrange apples and sausage in prepared baking dish.

3. Combine honey, water and cinnamon in medium bowl; mix well. Pour over apples and sausage. Dot with butter.

4. Bake 40 minutes, basting with pan juices occasionally, until apples are softened. *Makes 5 main-dish or 8 side-dish servings*

Lemon Shrimp

Aimee Dillman | Midlothian, Illinois

1 package (12 ounces) uncooked egg noodles
½ cup (1 stick) butter, softened
2 pounds cooked shrimp
3 tomatoes, chopped
1 cup chicken broth
1 cup shredded carrots
1 can (4 ounces) sliced mushrooms, drained
2 tablespoons fresh lemon juice
2 cloves garlic, chopped
½ teaspoon celery seed
¼ teaspoon black pepper

1. Preheat oven to 350°F.

2. Cook noodles according to package directions. Drain and mix with butte in large bowl, stirring until butter is melted and noodles are evenly coated. Add remaining ingredients and mix again. Transfer to 3-quart casserole.

3. Bake 15 to 20 minutes or until heated through.

Makes 8 servings

Home Cook's HINT

Room temperature lemons will yield more juice than those right out of the refrigerator. Roll lemons back and forth on a hard surface applying downward pressure with your hand to break up the pulp and make them easier to juice. If you need to juice cold lemons, use the microwave to warm them first. Microwave at HIGH for 20 seconds.

Hawaiian Pork Chops
Brenda Imler | Reddick, Florida

1 can (20 ounces) crushed pineapple, undrained
2 large sweet potatoes, peeled and sliced
1 teaspoon cinnamon
6 to 8 boneless pork chops
½ teaspoon salt
½ teaspoon pepper

1. Preheat oven to 350°F. Grease 13×9-inch casserole.

2. Place crushed pineapple in prepared casserole. Layer sweet potatoes over pineapple and sprinkle with cinnamon. Place pork chops on top and sprinkle with salt and pepper.

3. Cover with foil and bake about 1 hour or until sweet potatoes are tender and pork chops are tender and barely pink in center. Remove from oven. Increase oven temperature to 400°F. Remove foil and return casserole to oven. Bake about 10 minutes more until liquid is reduced and chops are browned. *Makes 6 to 8 servings*

Scallop & Artichoke Heart Casserole

1 package (9 ounces) frozen artichoke hearts, cooked and drained
1 pound scallops
1 teaspoon vegetable oil
¼ cup chopped red bell pepper
¼ cup sliced green onion tops
¼ cup all-purpose flour
2 cups 1% lowfat milk
1 teaspoon dried tarragon leaves, crushed
¼ teaspoon salt
¼ teaspoon white pepper
1 tablespoon chopped fresh parsley
Dash paprika

1. Cut large artichoke hearts lengthwise into halves. Arrange artichoke hearts in even layer in 8-inch square baking dish.

2. Rinse scallops; pat dry with paper towel. If scallops are large, cut into halves. Arrange scallops evenly over artichokes.

3. Preheat oven to 350°F. Heat oil in medium saucepan over medium-low heat. Add bell pepper and green onions; cook and stir 5 minutes or until tender. Stir in flour. Gradually stir in milk until smooth. Add tarragon, salt and white pepper; cook and stir over medium heat 10 minutes or until sauce boils and thickens.

4. Pour sauce over scallops. Bake, uncovered, 25 minutes or until bubbling and scallops are opaque. Sprinkle with chopped parsley and paprika before serving.   *Makes 4 servings*

Aunt Fran's Chicken and Rice
Lynda McCormick | Burkburnett, Texas

    2 cans (10¾ ounces each) condensed cream of onion soup,
       undiluted
 1½ cups uncooked rice
    6 skinless boneless chicken breasts (about 2 pounds) or other
       chicken pieces
    2 cans (10¾ ounces each) condensed reduced-fat, reduced-sodium
       cream of mushroom soup, undiluted
    1 can (4 ounces) sliced mushrooms, drained
    2 cups white wine

1. Preheat oven to 350°F.

2. Combine onion soup and rice in 13×9-inch baking dish; spread evenly to cover bottom of dish. Place chicken breasts on rice mixture, cover with mushroom soup and top with mushrooms. Pour wine evenly over all.

3. Bake uncovered for 1½ to 2 hours or until cooked through and chicken is no longer pink in center.   *Makes 6 servings*

PASTA
PERFECT

Macaroni & Cheese with Bacon
Susan Richardson | Libertyville, Ilinois

     8 ounces uncooked rotini pasta (about 3 cups)
     2 tablespoons butter or margarine
     2 tablespoons all-purpose flour
    ¼ teaspoon salt
    ¼ teaspoon dry mustard
    ⅛ teaspoon black pepper
 1½ cups milk
     8 ounces (2 cups) shredded sharp Cheddar cheese
     8 ounces bacon, crisp-cooked and crumbled*
     2 medium tomatoes, sliced

You may substitute 1 cup of cubed cooked ham for the bacon.

1. Preheat oven to 350°F. Lightly grease 1½-quart shallow casserole.

2. Cook pasta according to package directions; drain and return to saucepan.

3. Melt butter over medium-low heat in 2-quart saucepan. Whisk in flour, salt, mustard and pepper; cook and stir 1 minute. Whisk in milk. Bring to a boil over medium heat, stirring frequently. Reduce heat and simmer 2 minutes. Remove from heat. Add cheese; stir until melted.

4. Add cheese mixture and bacon to pasta; stir until well blended. Transfer to prepared casserole. Bake uncovered 20 minutes. Arrange tomato slices on casserole. Bake 5 to 8 minutes more or until casserole is bubbly and tomatoes are hot. *Makes 4 servings*

Macaroni & Cheese with Bacon 169

Pesto Lasagna

Karen Jensen | Evanston, Illinois

    1 package (16 ounces) lasagna noodles
    3 tablespoons olive oil
1½ cups chopped onion
    3 cloves garlic, finely chopped
    3 packages (10 ounces each) frozen chopped spinach, thawed,
        squeezed dry
    3 cups (about 24 ounces) ricotta cheese
1½ cups prepared pesto sauce
    ½ cup pine nuts, toasted
    ¾ cup (3 ounces) grated Parmesan cheese
    4 cups (16 ounces) shredded mozzarella cheese
        Strips of roasted red pepper (optional)

1. Preheat oven to 350°F. Oil 13×9-inch casserole or lasagna pan. Partially cook lasagna noodles according to package directions.

2. Heat oil in large skillet. Cook and stir onion and garlic until transparent. Add spinach and cook and stir about 5 minutes. Season with salt and pepper. Transfer to large bowl.

3. Add ricotta cheese, Parmesan cheese, pesto and pine nuts to spinach mixture; mix well.

4. Layer 5 lasagna noodles, slightly overlapping, in prepared casserole. Top with ⅓ of spinach-ricotta mixture, and ⅓ of mozzarella. Repeat layers twice.

5. Bake about 35 minutes until hot and bubbly. Garnish with red pepper, if desired. *Makes 8 servings*

Manicotti

Billie Olofson | Des Moines, Iowa

1 container (16 ounces) ricotta cheese
2 cups (8 ounces) shredded mozzarella cheese
½ cup cottage cheese
2 tablespoons grated Parmesan cheese
2 eggs, beaten
½ teaspoon minced garlic
   Salt and pepper
1 package (about 8 ounces) uncooked manicotti shells
1 pound ground beef
1 jar (26 ounces) spaghetti sauce
2 cups water

1. Combine ricotta cheese, mozzarella cheese, cottage cheese, Parmesan cheese, eggs and garlic in large bowl; mix well. Season with salt and pepper.

2. Stuff mixture into uncooked manicotti shells using rubber spatula. Place filled shells in 13×9-inch baking dish. Preheat oven to 375°F.

3. Cook ground beef in large skillet over medium-high heat until no longer pink, stirring to separate. Drain off excess fat. Stir in spaghetti sauce and water (mixture will be thin). Pour sauce over filled manicotti shells.

4. Cover with foil; bake 1 hour or until sauce has thickened and shells are tender. *Makes 6 servings*

Home Cook's HINT

It's much easier to stuff uncooked pasta shells than boiled ones. As long as the pasta is covered with enough liquid, it will cook right in the sauce in the oven and save the step of boiling it first. Many lasagna recipes can also be prepared with uncooked lasagna noodles.

Corned Beef Casserole

Barbara Gosen | Tucson, Arizona

1 package (8 ounces) uncooked wide egg noodles
3 cups shredded Mexican cheese blend, divided
1 can (12 ounces) corned beef
1 can (10¾ ounces) condensed cream of chicken or cream of
    mushroom soup, undiluted
1 cup milk
½ cup chopped onion
½ cup French fried onions

1. Preheat oven to 350°F. Cook egg noodles according to package directions. Drain and keep warm.

2. Combine 2½ cups cheese, corned beef, soup, milk and chopped onion in large bowl. Add cooked noodles; mix well.

3. Transfer to 3- or 4-quart casserole; top with remaining ½ cup cheese. Sprinkle with French fried onions.

4. Bake, uncovered, 45 minutes or until hot and bubbly.

Makes 6 to 8 servings

Cheesy Chicken Spaghetti

Janeice Burnett | Fontana, California

5 boneless skinless chicken breasts, diced
1 bottle (12 ounces) Worcestershire sauce
2 tablespoons oil
1 pound (16 ounces) spaghetti, cooked and drained
1 jar (about 26 ounces) spaghetti sauce
1 cup chopped onion
4 cups (16 ounces) shredded Cheddar cheese

1. Preheat oven to 350°F. Combine chicken and Worcestershire sauce in large bowl and toss to coat. Cover, refrigerate and marinate 5 hours, stirring mixture every hour.

2. Preheat oven to 350°F. Spray 4-quart casserole with nonstick cooking spray. Heat oil in Dutch oven over medium-high heat. Drain chicken and discard marinade. Add chicken to Dutch oven and cook until no longer pink in center. Add cooked spaghetti, spaghetti sauce and onion; cook and stir until heated through.

3. Transfer spaghetti mixture to prepared casserole; top with cheese.

4. Bake 20 to 25 minutes or until cheese is melted and golden brown.

Makes 5 servings

Pasta & White Bean Casserole

Julie DeMatteo | Clementon, New Jersey

½ cup chopped onion
2 cloves garlic, minced
1 tablespoon olive oil
2 cans (about 15 ounces each) cannellini beans, drained and rinsed
3 cups cooked small shell pasta
1 can (8 ounces) tomato sauce
1½ teaspoons dried Italian seasoning
½ teaspoon salt
½ teaspoon pepper
1 cup (4 ounces) shredded Italian cheese blend
2 tablespoons finely chopped parsley

1. Preheat oven to 350°F. Spray 2-quart casserole with nonstick cooking spray. Cook onion and garlic in oil in large skillet over medium-high heat 3 to 4 minutes or until onion is tender.

2. Add beans, pasta, tomato sauce, Italian seasoning, salt and pepper; mix well. Transfer to prepared casserole; sprinkle with cheese and parsley. Bake 20 minutes or until cheese is melted.

Makes 6 servings

Cousin Arlene's Spaghetti Lasagna

Arlene Vanderbilt | Palos Heights, Illinois

8 ounces uncooked spaghetti or other thin pasta
1 clove garlic, finely chopped
1 tablespoon butter
2 pounds lean ground beef
1 teaspoon sugar
   Salt and pepper
2 cans (8 ounces each) tomato sauce
1 can (6 ounces) tomato paste
1 small package (3 ounces) cream cheese, softened
1 cup (8 ounces) sour cream
6 green onions, chopped
¼ cup (2 ounces) grated Parmesan cheese

1. Preheat oven to 350°F. Boil spaghetti in large saucepan of salted boiling water until almost tender. Drain and reserve.

2. Heat butter in large skillet over medium heat. Add garlic; cook and stir 1 minute. Add ground beef and sugar; season with salt and pepper. Cook and stir until beef is no longer pink; drain fat. Add tomato sauce and tomato paste; simmer 20 minutes, stirring occasionally.

3. Meanwhile blend cream cheese and sour cream in medium bowl until smooth. Add green onions and mix well.

4. Spread a little meat sauce in 2-quart casserole to prevent noodles from sticking. Layer ½ of spaghetti, ½ of sour cream mixture and ½ of meat mixture. Repeat layers. Sprinkle on Parmesan cheese. Bake 35 minutes or until heated through.   *Makes 6 servings*

Arlene says: This casserole can be frozen and baked later, however, thaw it in the refrigerator overnight and let it come to room temperature before baking. I always double this recipe since it makes great leftovers.

Bow Tie Zucchini

Karen Tellier | Cumberland, Rhode Island

¼ cup vegetable oil
1 cup chopped onion
2 cloves garlic, minced
5 small zucchini, cut into thin strips
⅔ cup heavy cream
1 package (16 ounces) bow tie pasta, cooked and drained
3 tablespoons grated Parmesan cheese
Salt and pepper

1. Preheat oven to 350°F.

2. Heat oil in large skillet over medium-high heat. Add onion and garlic; cook and stir until onion is tender. Add zucchini; cook and stir until tender.

3. Add cream; cook and stir until thickened. Add pasta and cheese to skillet. Season with salt and pepper to taste. Transfer mixture to 2-quart casserole. Cover and bake 15 minutes or until heated through.

Makes 8 servings

Home Cook's HINT

To quickly peel a garlic clove, place it on a cutting board. Slightly crush the clove under the flat side of a chef's knife blade. The skin will easily peel away. To make chopping garlic easier, sprinkle the peeled cloves with a bit of salt and the garlic won't stick to your knife as much.

Fresh Vegetable Lasagna

8 ounces uncooked lasagna noodles
1 package (10 ounces) frozen chopped spinach, thawed and well
    drained
1 cup shredded carrots
½ cup sliced green onions
½ cup sliced red bell pepper
¼ cup chopped fresh parsley
½ teaspoon black pepper
1½ cups low-fat cottage cheese
1 cup buttermilk
½ cup plain nonfat yogurt
2 egg whites
1 cup sliced mushrooms
1 can (14 ounces) artichoke hearts, drained and chopped
1½ cups (8 ounces) shredded part-skim mozzarella cheese, divided
¼ cup freshly grated Parmesan cheese

1. Cook pasta according to package directions, omitting salt. Drain. Rinse under cold water; drain well. Set aside.

2. Preheat oven to 375°F. Pat spinach with paper towels to remove excess moisture. Combine spinach, carrots, green onions, bell pepper, parsley and black pepper in large bowl. Set aside.

3. Combine cottage cheese, buttermilk, yogurt and egg whites in food processor or blender; process until smooth.

4. Spray 13×9-inch baking pan with nonstick cooking spray. Arrange a third of lasagna noodles in bottom of pan. Spread with ½ cottage cheese mixture, ½ vegetable mixture, ½ mushrooms, ½ artichokes and ³/₄ cup mozzarella. Repeat layers, ending with noodles. Sprinkle with remaining ½ cup mozzarella and Parmesan.

5. Cover and bake 30 minutes. Remove cover; continue baking 20 minutes or until bubbly and heated through. Let stand 10 minutes before serving. *Makes 8 servings*

Fresh Vegetable Lasagna

Ravioli Casserole

Carrie Mae Anderson | Hyattsville, Maryland

1 pound lean ground beef
2 tablespoons dried onion flakes
2 teaspoons soy sauce
¼ teaspoon dried minced garlic
2 packages (10 ounces each) frozen chopped spinach, thawed and
　　drained
1 jar (26 ounces) prepared spaghetti sauce
1 can (8 ounces) tomato sauce
1 can (6 ounces) tomato paste
1 tablespoon barbecue sauce
1 teaspoon Italian salad dressing
½ teaspoon dried oregano
¼ teaspoon pepper
1 package (7 ounces) macaroni, cooked and drained
2 cups (8 ounces) shredded sharp Cheddar cheese
½ cup bread crumbs
2 eggs, beaten
¼ cup vegetable oil

1. Preheat oven to 350°F. Spray 13×9-inch casserole with nonstick cooking spray. Cook ground beef, onion, soy sauce and garlic in large skillet over medium heat 5 minutes or until no longer pink. Stir in spinach, spaghetti sauce, tomato sauce, tomato paste, barbecue sauce, salad dressing, oregano and pepper. Reduce heat to low; simmer 10 minutes.

2. Combine cooked macaroni, cheese, bread crumbs, eggs and oil in large bowl; mix well. Spread evenly in bottom of prepared casserole; top with beef mixture.

3. Bake 30 minutes or until hot and bubbly.

Makes 8 to 10 servings

Penne Chicken Casserole

Yuki Mountjoy | *Des Moines, Washington*

1½ pounds boneless skinless chicken breasts
3 cups water
2 cubes beef bouillon
4 cups cooked penne pasta
1 can (10¾ ounces) condensed cream of chicken soup, undiluted
1 cup sour cream
½ cup grated Asiago cheese
½ cup mayonnaise
⅓ cup dry sherry
½ cup dry Italian-seasoned bread crumbs
¼ cup grated Parmesan cheese
¼ cup margarine or butter, melted

1. Preheat oven to 350°F. Spray 2-quart casserole with nonstick cooking spray. Place chicken, water and bouillon cubes in large saucepan over medium heat. Cook 20 minutes or until chicken is no longer pink in center. Drain liquid and discard; cut chicken into cubes. Combine pasta and chicken in prepared casserole.

2. Combine soup, sour cream, Asiago cheese, mayonnaise and sherry in medium bowl; mix well. Spoon evenly over pasta and chicken.

3. Toss bread crumbs, Parmesan cheese and margarine in small bowl. Sprinkle over casserole. Bake 30 to 45 minutes or until golden brown.

Makes 6 servings

Home Cook's HINT

If you end up with leftover cooked pasta, save it for another use. Drain the part you're not using immediately and put it in ice water for a few seconds to stop further cooking. Drain thoroughly and toss the pasta with a teaspoon or two of oil to prevent it from sticking together and refrigerate, covered, for up to three days.

Italian Tomato Bake

Terry Lunday | Flagstaff, Arizona

1 pound sweet Italian sausage, cut into ½-inch slices
2 tablespoons margarine or butter
1 cup chopped onion
4 cups cooked egg noodles
2 cups prepared spaghetti sauce
2 cups frozen broccoli florets
½ cup diced tomatoes
2 cloves garlic, minced
3 Roma tomatoes, sliced
1 cup (8 ounces) low-fat ricotta cheese
⅓ cup grated Parmesan cheese
1 teaspoon dried oregano leaves

1. Preheat oven to 350°F. Cook sausage in skillet over medium heat about 10 minutes or until barely pink in center. Remove, drain on paper towels and reserve. Drain fat from skillet.

2. Add margarine and onion to skillet; cook and stir until onion is tender. Meanwhile, steam broccoli 5 minutes until crisp-tender; drain. Combine onion, noodles, pasta sauce, broccoli, diced tomatoes and garlic in large bowl; mix well.

3. Transfer to 13×9-inch baking dish. Top with cooked sausage and arrange tomato slices over top. Place 1 heaping tablespoon ricotta cheese on each tomato slice. Sprinkle casserole with Parmesan cheese and oregano. Bake 35 minutes or until hot and bubbly.

Makes 6 servings

Tuscan Baked Rigatoni

Julie DeMatteo | Clementon, New Jersey

1 pound Italian sausage, casings removed
1 pound rigatoni pasta, cooked, drained and kept warm
2 cups (8 ounces) shredded fontina cheese
2 tablespoons olive oil
2 fennel bulbs, thinly sliced
4 cloves garlic, minced
1 can (28 ounces) crushed tomatoes
1 cup heavy cream
1 teaspoon salt
1 teaspoon pepper
8 cups coarsely chopped spinach
1 can (15 ounces) cannellini beans, rinsed and drained
2 tablespoons pine nuts
½ cup grated Parmesan cheese

1. Preheat oven to 350°F. Spray 4-quart casserole with nonstick cooking spray. Crumble sausage in large skillet over medium-high heat. Cook and stir until no longer pink; drain. Transfer sausage to large bowl. Add cooked pasta and fontina cheese; mix well.

2. Combine oil, fennel and garlic in same skillet. Cook and stir over medium heat 3 minutes or until fennel is tender. Add tomatoes, cream, salt and pepper; cook and stir until slightly thickened. Stir in spinach, beans and pine nuts; cook until heated through.

3. Pour sauce over pasta and sausage; toss to coat. Transfer to prepared casserole; sprinkle evenly with Parmesan cheese. Bake 30 minutes or until heated through. *Makes 6 to 8 servings*

Tuscan Baked Rigatoni

Spinach Stuffed Manicotti

1 package (10 ounces) frozen spinach
8 uncooked manicotti shells
1½ teaspoons olive oil
1 teaspoon dried rosemary
1 teaspoon dried sage leaves
1 teaspoon dried oregano leaves
1 teaspoon dried thyme leaves
1 teaspoon chopped garlic
1½ cups chopped fresh tomatoes
½ cup ricotta cheese
½ cup fresh whole wheat bread crumbs
2 egg whites, lightly beaten
Yellow pepper rings and sage sprig for garnish

1. Cook spinach according to package directions. Place in colander to drain. Let stand until cool enough to handle. Squeeze spinach with hands to remove excess moisture. Set aside.

2. Cook pasta according to package directions, drain. Rinse under cold running water until cool enough to handle; drain.

3. Preheat oven to 350°F. Heat oil in medium saucepan over medium heat. Cook and stir rosemary, sage, oregano, thyme and garlic in hot oil about 1 minute. Do not let herbs turn brown. Add tomatoes; reduce heat to low. Simmer, uncovered, 10 minutes, stirring occasionally.

4. Combine spinach, cheese and crumbs in bowl. Fold in egg whites. Fill shells with spinach mixture using spoon.

5. Place one third of tomato mixture on bottom of 13×9-inch baking pan. Arrange manicotti in pan. Pour remaining tomato mixture over top. Cover with foil.

6. Bake 30 minutes or until bubbly. Garnish, if desired.

Makes 4 servings

Spinach Stuffed Manicotti

Rigatoni à la Vodka

Jenni Smith | Feasterville, Pennsylvania

1 pound ground beef
1 jar (26 ounces) prepared spaghetti sauce
1½ cups (12 ounces) 3-cheese pasta sauce
4 cups (16 ounces) shredded mozzarella and Cheddar cheese blend, divided
6 tablespoons vodka
12 ounces rigatoni pasta, cooked and drained

1. Preheat oven to 350°F. Spray 3-quart casserole with nonstick cooking spray. Cook ground beef in medium skillet over medium heat 5 minutes or until no longer pink; drain excess fat. Add pasta sauces, 2 cups cheese and vodka. Cook and stir until heated through.

2. Place cooked pasta in prepared casserole. Pour vodka sauce evenly over pasta; sprinkle with remaining 2 cups cheese.

3. Bake 15 minutes or until cheese has melted.   *Makes 4 servings*

Crunchy Tuna Casserole

Carol Galbreath | Avon, Indiana

1 can (10¾ ounces) condensed cream of chicken soup, undiluted
6 ounces medium noodles or macaroni, cooked and drained
1 can (6 ounces) tuna, drained and flaked
1 cup (4 ounces) shredded sharp Cheddar cheese
½ cup sliced celery
½ cup milk
¼ cup mayonnaise
1 can (4 ounces) sliced water chestnuts, drained
1 jar (2 ounces) chopped pimientos, drained
½ teaspoon salt
Dash pepper
Pinch celery seeds

1. Preheat oven to 425°F. Spray 2-quart casserole with nonstick cooking spray.

2. Combine all ingredients in prepared casserole. Bake 25 minutes or until hot and bubbly. *Makes 6 servings*

Mom's Baked Mostaccioli
Lynda McCormick | *Burkburnett, Texas*

1 container (16 ounces) part-skim ricotta cheese
½ cup egg substitute
¼ cup grated Parmesan cheese
  Garlic powder
  Pepper
  Italian seasoning
1 package (16 ounces) mostaccioli, cooked and drained
1 jar (26 ounces) prepared spaghetti sauce
1½ cups (6 ounces) shredded mozzarella cheese

1. Preheat oven to 350°F. Spray 13×9-inch casserole with nonstick cooking spray.

2. Combine ricotta cheese, egg substitute and Parmesan cheese in medium bowl. Season with garlic powder, pepper and Italian seasoning; mix well.

3. Place half of pasta in prepared casserole. Spread ricotta mixture evenly over pasta. Spoon remaining pasta over ricotta mixture. Top with spaghetti sauce and mozzarella cheese.

4. Bake 30 minutes or until hot and bubbly. *Makes 8 servings*

ONE-DISH
DINNERS

Lickety-Split Paella Pronto!
Janice Elder | Charlotte, North Carolina

1 tablespoon olive oil
1 large onion, chopped
2 cloves garlic, minced
1 jar (16 ounces) salsa
1 can (14½ ounces) diced peeled tomatoes, undrained
1 can (14 ounces) artichoke hearts, drained and quartered
1 can (14 ounces) chicken broth
1 package (about 8 ounces) yellow rice
1 can (12 ounces) solid white tuna, drained and flaked
1 package (9 to 10 ounces) frozen green peas
2 tablespoons finely chopped green onions (optional)
2 tablespoons finely chopped red bell pepper (optional)

1. Heat oil in large nonstick skillet over medium heat until hot. Add onion and garlic; cook and stir about 5 minutes or until onion is tender.

2. Stir in salsa, tomatoes, artichokes, chicken broth and rice. Bring to a boil. Cover; reduce heat to low and simmer 15 minutes.

3. Stir in tuna and peas. Cover; cook 5 to 10 minutes or until rice is tender and tuna and peas are heated through. Sprinkle each serving with green onions and red bell pepper, if desired.

Makes 4 to 6 servings

City Chicken BBQ Casserole
Jan Blue | Cuyahoga Falls, Ohio

2 tablespoons vegetable oil
6 to 8 boneless pork* chops (about 2 pounds), cut into bite-size pieces
¼ cup chopped onions
2 cloves garlic, chopped
2 cups water
2 cups uncooked instant white rice
2 cups shredded mozzarella cheese

"City chicken" is a traditional dish in Ohio and Pennsylvania. The name indicates that chicken was once more expensive than pork, so the cheaper cuts of pork were prepared to taste like chicken.

Sauce:

1 bottle (12 ounces) chili sauce
1 cup ketchup
½ cup packed brown sugar
2 tablespoons honey
1 tablespoon Worcestershire sauce
1 tablespoon hot pepper jelly
1 teaspoon ground ginger
1 teaspoon liquid smoke (optional)
½ teaspoon curry powder
¼ teaspoon black pepper

1. Preheat oven to 350°F.

2. Heat oil in large skillet over medium-high heat until hot. Add pork; cook and stir 10 to 15 minutes or until browned and no longer pink in center. Add onions and garlic; cook until onions are tender. Drain fat.

3. Meanwhile, bring water to a boil in small saucepan. Stir in rice; cover. Remove from heat; let stand 5 minutes or until water is absorbed.

4. Combine sauce ingredients in separate saucepan; bring to a boil. Reduce heat to low; cover and simmer 10 minutes, stirring occasionally.

5. Combine pork mixture, rice and sauce in 2½-quart casserole; mix well. Bake 15 to 20 minutes. Top with mozzarella cheese and bake 5 minutes more. Serve hot. *Makes 6 to 8 servings*

3rd Prize Winner

City Chicken BBQ Casserole 195

Potato Sausage Casserole

Billie Olofson | Des Moines, Iowa

1 pound pork sausage or ground pork
1 can (10¾ ounces) condensed cream of mushroom soup, undiluted
¾ cup milk
½ cup chopped onion
½ teaspoon salt
¼ teaspoon black pepper
3 cups sliced potatoes, uncooked
½ tablespoon butter
1½ cups (6 ounces) shredded Cheddar cheese

1. Preheat oven to 350°F. Spray 1½-quart casserole with nonstick cooking spray; set aside.

2. Cook meat in large skillet over medium-high heat until no longer pink; drain fat.

3. Stir together soup, milk, onion, salt and pepper in medium bowl.

4. Place ½ of potatoes in bottom of prepared casserole; top with ½ of soup mixture, then with ½ of sausage. Repeat layers, ending with sausage. Dot with butter.

4. Cover pan with foil. Bake 1¼ to 1½ hours until potatoes are tender. Uncover; sprinkle with cheese. Return to oven; bake until cheese is melted and bubbly. *Makes 6 servings*

Ham Jambalaya

Margaret Pache | Mesa, Arizona

2 tablespoons butter
1 large onion, chopped
½ cup thinly sliced celery
½ red bell pepper, diced
2 cloves garlic, minced
1 jar (about 16 ounces) medium-hot salsa
2 cups cubed cooked ham
1 cup uncooked long-grain rice
1 cup water
⅔ cup vegetable broth
3 teaspoons extra-hot horseradish
2 teaspoons honey
¼ to ½ teaspoon hot pepper sauce
1½ pounds shrimp, peeled and deveined
1 tablespoon chopped fresh mint

1. Preheat oven to 350°F.

2. Melt butter in 3-quart Dutch oven over medium heat. Add onion, celery, bell pepper and garlic. Cook about 2 minutes or until vegetables are tender.

3. Add all remaining ingredients except shrimp and mint. Bake, covered, about 40 minutes or until rice is almost tender.

4. Remove from oven and stir in shrimp and mint. Return to oven and bake additional 10 to 15 minutes or until shrimp are opaque.

Makes 6 to 8 servings

Crab, Shrimp & Zucchini Baked Delight

Louise A Donavant | Bellevue, Washington

- 2 medium zucchini
- 1 cup flaked fresh crab
- 1 cup small fresh bay shrimp
- 1 cup sour cream
- ⅓ cup sliced green pimento-stuffed olives
- 1 tablespoon finely chopped onion
- 1 tablespoon finely chopped green bell pepper
- 1 tablespoon fresh lemon juice
- 2 cups (8 ounces) shredded Cheddar cheese
- Paprika and parsley sprigs, for garnish (optional)

1. Preheat oven to 300°F. Butter 8×10-inch baking dish

2. Place zucchini in saucepan of boiling water. Boil 3 to 5 minutes or until crisp-tender. Cool slightly. Cut zucchinis in half lengthwise. Scoop out seeds and some of flesh; discard seeds and flesh. Place in prepared baking dish, hollow side up.

3. Combine crab, shrimp, sour cream, olives, onion, bell pepper and lemon juice in large bowl; mix well. Place ¼ of crab mixture in each zucchini half. Top each zucchini half with ½ cup cheese.

4. Bake 1 hour or until lightly browned. Garnish with paprika and parsley sprigs, if desired. *Makes 4 servings*

Salmon Casserole

Sandra Marie Swift | *Pensacola, Florida*

2 tablespoons margarine or butter
2 cups sliced mushrooms
1½ cups chopped carrots
1 cup frozen peas
1 cup chopped celery
½ cup chopped onion
½ cup chopped red bell pepper
1 clove garlic, minced
1 teaspoon salt
½ teaspoon black pepper
1 tablespoon chopped fresh parsley
½ teaspoon dried basil leaves
4 cups cooked rice
1 can (14 ounces) red salmon, drained and flaked
1 can (10¾ ounces) condensed cream of mushroom soup, undiluted
12 cups (8 ounces) grated Cheddar or American cheese
½ cup sliced black olives

1. Preheat oven to 350°F. Spray 2-quart casserole with nonstick cooking spray; set aside.

2. Melt margarine in large skillet or Dutch oven over medium heat. Add mushrooms, carrots, peas, celery, onion, bell pepper, garlic, salt, pepper, parsley and basil; cook and stir 10 minutes or until vegetables are tender. Add rice, salmon, soup and cheese; mix well.

3. Transfer to prepared casserole. Sprinkle olives over top. Bake 30 minutes or until hot and bubbly. *Makes 8 servings*

Easy Moroccan Casserole

April Parmelee | Anaheim, California

2 tablespoons vegetable oil
1 pound pork stew meat, cut into 1-inch cubes
½ cup chopped onion
3 tablespoons all-purpose flour
1 can (16 ounces) diced tomatoes, undrained
¼ cup water
1 teaspoon ground ginger
1 teaspoon ground cumin
1 teaspoon ground cinnamon
½ teaspoon sugar
½ teaspoon salt
½ teaspoon black pepper
2 medium red potatoes, unpeeled, cut into ½-inch pieces
1 large sweet potato, unpeeled, cut into ½-inch pieces
1 cup frozen lima beans, thawed and drained
1 cup frozen cut green beans, thawed and drained
¾ cup sliced carrots
Pita bread

1. Preheat oven to 325°F.

2. Heat oil in large skillet over medium-high heat. Add pork and onion; cook, stirring occasionally, until pork is browned on all sides.

3. Sprinkle flour over meat mixture in skillet. Stir until flour has absorbed pan juices. Cook 2 minutes more.

4. Stir in tomatoes with juice, water, ginger, cumin, cinnamon, sugar, salt and pepper. Transfer mixture to 2-quart casserole. Bake 30 minutes.

5. Stir in potatoes, sweet potato, lima beans, green beans, and carrots. Cover and bake 1 hour or until potatoes are tender. Serve with pita bread. *Makes 6 servings*

Honorable Mention Winner

Beef in Wine Sauce

Tamara Frazier | Escondido, California

4 pounds boneless beef chuck, cut into 1½- to 2-inch cubes
2 tablespoons garlic powder
2 cans (10¾ ounces each) condensed golden mushroom soup, undiluted
1 envelope (about 1 ounce) onion soup mix
¾ cup dry sherry
1 can (8 ounces) sliced mushrooms, drained
1 bag (20 ounces) frozen sliced carrots

1. Preheat oven to 325°F. Spray heavy 4-quart casserole or Dutch oven with nonstick cooking spray.

2. Sprinkle beef with garlic powder. Place in casserole.

3. Combine mushroom soup, onion soup mix, sherry and mushrooms in medium bowl. Pour over meat; mix well.

4. Cover casserole and bake 3 hours or until meat is very tender. Add carrots during last 15 minutes of baking.   *Makes 6 to 8 servings*

Home Cook's HINT

Cooking a tough cut of meat, like beef chuck, for a long time at low heat with a little liquid is often called braising. It is a good method for getting maximum flavor and tenderness from less expensive cuts. For best results, braise in a sturdy, heavy casserole that retains heat and spreads it evenly through the contents.

Tuna-Macaroni Casserole

Andrée Tracey | St. Louis Park, Minnesota

1 cup mayonnaise
1 cup (4 ounces) shredded Swiss cheese
½ cup milk
¼ cup chopped onion
¼ cup chopped sweet red bell pepper or pimiento
⅛ teaspoon black pepper
2 cans (7 ounces each) tuna, drained and flaked
1 package (about 10 ounces) frozen peas
2 cups shell pasta or elbow macaroni, cooked and drained
½ cup dry bread crumbs, optional
2 tablespoons melted butter or corn oil (optional)

1. Preheat oven to 350°F.

2. Stir together mayonnaise, cheese, milk, onion, red pepper and black pepper in large bowl. Add tuna, peas and macaroni, toss to coat well.

3. Spoon into 2-qt. casserole. If desired, mix bread crumbs with butter in small bowl and sprinkle on top. Bake 30 to 40 minutes or until heated through. *Makes 6 servings*

Andrée says: This casserole freezes extremely well. Just mix up the ingredients, except for the bread crumb topping, and stir thoroughly. You don't even have to thaw the peas. Then spoon the mixture into storage containers (1 big one or 6 individual size) and freeze until you're ready to bake.

Carmel Chicken Fresco Bake

Elaine Sweet | Dallas, Texas

        4 cups broccoli florets
        4 tablespoons butter, divided
       12 ounces baby portobello mushrooms, sliced
        3 shallots, diced
        1 can (14 ounces) artichoke hearts, rinsed, drained and quartered
        4 tablespoons all-purpose flour
     2½ cups chicken broth
        1 teaspoon Dijon mustard
        ½ teaspoon salt
        ½ teaspoon dried tarragon leaves
        ½ teaspoon black pepper
        1 cup grated Emmentaler cheese
        2 pounds boneless skinless chicken breasts, cooked and cut into
            1½-inch cubes
        ¼ cup grated Asiago cheese

1. Preheat oven to 350°F. Spray 4-quart baking dish with nonstick cooking spray; set aside.

2. Steam broccoli about 6 minutes or until tender. Rinse and drain under cold water. Set aside.

3. Melt 1 tablespoon butter in medium skillet over medium heat. Add mushrooms and shallots; cook and stir about 5 minutes or until soft. Remove from skillet and combine with broccoli in large bowl. Stir in artichoke hearts.

4. Melt remaining 3 tablespoons butter in same skillet. Blend in flour. Add chicken broth, mustard, salt, tarragon and pepper; whisk about 2 minutes or until sauce thickens. Add Emmantaler cheese and stir until smooth.

5. Alternately layer chicken and vegetable mixture in baking dish. Pour cheese sauce over top of casserole. Cover with foil and bake 40 minutes. Remove foil; sprinkle casserole with Asiago cheese. Bake 5 to 10 minutes or until cheese melts.   *Makes 8 servings*

Tuna Tomato Casserole

Cortney Morford | Tuckahoe, New Jersey

2 cans (6 ounces each) tuna, drained
1 cup mayonnaise
1 small onion, finely chopped
¼ teaspoon salt
¼ teaspoon black pepper
1 bag (12 ounces) uncooked wide egg noodles
8 to 10 plum tomatoes, sliced ¼ inch thick
1 cup (4 ounces) shredded Cheddar or mozzarella cheese

1. Preheat oven to 375°F.

1. Combine tuna, mayonnaise, onion, salt and pepper in medium bowl. Mix well and set aside.

2. Prepare noodles according to package directions, cooking just until tender. Drain noodles and return to pot.

3. Add tuna mixture to noodles; stir until well combined.

4. Layer ½ noodle mixture, ½ tomatoes and ½ cheese in 13×9-inch baking dish. Press down slightly. Repeat layers with remaining ingredients.

5. Bake 20 minutes or until cheese is melted and casserole is heated through. *Makes 6 servings*

Seafood Newburg Casserole

Julie De Matteo | Clementon, New Jersey

1 can (10¾ ounces) condensed cream of shrimp soup, undiluted
½ cup half-and-half
1 tablespoon dry sherry
¼ teaspoon ground red pepper
3 cups cooked rice
2 cans (6 ounces each) lump crabmeat, drained
¼ pound medium shrimp, peeled and deveined
¼ pound bay scallops
1 jar (4 ounces) pimientos, drained and chopped
¼ cup finely chopped parsley

1. Preheat oven to 350°F. Spray 2½-quart casserole with nonstick cooking spray.

2. Whisk together soup, half-and-half, sherry and red pepper in large bowl until combined. Add rice, crab, shrimp, scallops and pimientos; toss well.

3. Transfer to prepared casserole; sprinkle with parsley. Cover and bake about 25 minutes or until shrimp and scallops are opaque.

Makes 6 servings

Home Cook's HINT

Always pick over crabmeat carefully to make sure there are no tiny pieces of shell or cartilage. Taste canned crabmeat before using it. If there is a metallic flavor, soak it in ice water for 5 minutes. Then drain and blot dry.

Seafood Newburg Casserole   211

Thyme for Chicken Stew
with Polenta Dumplings

Diane Halferty | *Corpus Christi, Texas*

2 pounds boneless skinless chicken thighs
4 tablespoons olive oil, divided
2 medium eggplants, chopped
6 small onions, chopped
4 tomatoes, seeded and diced
½ cup chicken broth
⅓ cup pitted black olives, sliced
1 tablespoon chopped fresh thyme *or* 1 teaspoon dried thyme leaves
1 tablespoon red wine vinegar
Dumplings (recipe page 214)

1. Preheat oven to 350°F.

2. Rinse chicken and pat dry with paper towels. Heat 1 tablespoon oil over medium-high heat in 4-quart Dutch oven. Cook chicken in batches 4 to 5 minutes or until browned on all sides. Remove and set aside.

3. Heat remaining 3 tablespoons oil in same Dutch oven; add eggplant, onions and tomatoes. Reduce heat to medium. Cook, stirring occasionally, 5 minutes. Return chicken to Dutch oven. Add chicken broth, olives, thyme and vinegar; stir to combine. Bring to a boil. Transfer to oven; bake uncovered 1 hour. Meanwhile, prepare Dumplings.

4. Remove stew from oven; top with rounded tablespoonfuls dumpling mixture. Bake uncovered about 20 minutes or until dumplings are cooked through. *Makes 6 servings*

Continued on page 214

Thyme for Chicken Stew with Polenta Dumplings   213

Thyme for Chicken Stew with Polenta Dumplings continued from page 212

Dumplings

3½ cups chicken broth
1 cup polenta or yellow cornmeal
1 large egg, beaten
2 tablespoons butter
½ cup grated Parmesan cheese
¼ cup chopped fresh parsley

1. Bring broth to a boil in medium saucepan over medium-high heat. Gradually whisk in polenta. Reduce heat to low; simmer, stirring, about 15 minutes or until thickened.

2. Remove saucepan from heat; stir in egg, butter, cheese and parsley.

Makes 6 servings

Pizza Potato Casserole

Marie McConnell | Las Cruces, New Mexico

1 pound Italian sausage, casings removed
1 package (16 ounces) scalloped potato mix
1 can (14½ ounces) crushed tomatoes
2 cups sliced mushrooms
1½ cups water
1 teaspoon dried basil leaves
1 teaspoon dried oregano leaves
Salt
Black pepper
2 cups (8 ounces) shredded mozzarella cheese

1. Preheat oven to 400°F. Spray 3-quart casserole with nonstick cooking spray; set aside.

2. Cook sausage in large skillet over medium-high heat until no longer pink, stirring to separate meat. Add potatoes, tomatoes, mushrooms, water, basil, oregano, salt and pepper.

3. Transfer mixture to prepared casserole. Top with cheese. Bake 30 to 40 minutes or until cheese melts.

Makes 4 servings

Sunday Dinner Casserole

Ronda Tucker | Ten Mile, Tennessee

2 cups sweet onion rings
½ cup cooking sherry
2 tablespoons sugar
2 tablespoons balsamic vinegar
1 teaspoon dried thyme leaves
½ teaspoon freshly ground black pepper
2 cups egg noodles, cooked and drained
2 pounds boneless skinless chicken breasts
3 cups chicken broth
1 can (14½ ounces) diced tomatoes, drained
2 cloves garlic minced
½ teaspoon crushed red pepper
2 teaspoons grated lemon peel
¼ cup chopped fresh basil

1. Preheat oven to 400°F.

2. Combine onions, sherry, sugar, vinegar, thyme and black pepper in large skillet. Cook, stirring occasionally, over medium heat until onions begin to brown.

3. Meanwhile, place noodles in 13×9-inch baking pan. Top with chicken breasts. Combine broth, tomatoes, garlic and red pepper with onions in skillet. Pour over chicken-noodle mixture in baking pan.

4. Bake, uncovered, 20 minutes; turn chicken breasts. Bake additional 20 to 25 minutes or until chicken is no longer pink in center and juices run clear. Sprinkle with lemon peel and basil.

Makes 4 to 6 servings.

METRIC CONVERSION CHART

VOLUME MEASUREMENTS (dry)

1/8 teaspoon = 0.5 mL
1/4 teaspoon = 1 mL
1/2 teaspoon = 2 mL
3/4 teaspoon = 4 mL
1 teaspoon = 5 mL
1 tablespoon = 15 mL
2 tablespoons = 30 mL
1/4 cup = 60 mL
1/3 cup = 75 mL
1/2 cup = 125 mL
2/3 cup = 150 mL
3/4 cup = 175 mL
1 cup = 250 mL
2 cups = 1 pint = 500 mL
3 cups = 750 mL
4 cups = 1 quart = 1 L

VOLUME MEASUREMENTS (fluid)

1 fluid ounce (2 tablespoons) = 30 mL
4 fluid ounces (1/2 cup) = 125 mL
8 fluid ounces (1 cup) = 250 mL
12 fluid ounces (1 1/2 cups) = 375 mL
16 fluid ounces (2 cups) = 500 mL

WEIGHTS (mass)

1/2 ounce = 15 g
1 ounce = 30 g
3 ounces = 90 g
4 ounces = 120 g
8 ounces = 225 g
10 ounces = 285 g
12 ounces = 360 g
16 ounces = 1 pound = 450 g

DIMENSIONS

1/16 inch = 2 mm
1/8 inch = 3 mm
1/4 inch = 6 mm
1/2 inch = 1.5 cm
3/4 inch = 2 cm
1 inch = 2.5 cm

OVEN TEMPERATURES

250°F = 120°C
275°F = 140°C
300°F = 150°C
325°F = 160°C
350°F = 180°C
375°F = 190°C
400°F = 200°C
425°F = 220°C
450°F = 230°C

BAKING PAN SIZES

Utensil	Size in Inches/Quarts	Metric Volume	Size in Centimeters
Baking or Cake Pan (square or rectangular)	8×8×2	2 L	20×20×5
	9×9×2	2.5 L	23×23×5
	12×8×2	3 L	30×20×5
	13×9×2	3.5 L	33×23×5
Loaf Pan	8×4×3	1.5 L	20×10×7
	9×5×3	2 L	23×13×7
Round Layer Cake Pan	8×1 1/2	1.2 L	20×4
	9×1 1/2	1.5 L	23×4
Pie Plate	8×1 1/4	750 mL	20×3
	9×1 1/4	1 L	23×3
Baking Dish or Casserole	1 quart	1 L	—
	1 1/2 quart	1.5 L	—
	2 quart	2 L	—

Do you have your own favorite original recipe? We'd love to hear about it! Send it in, along with the submission form below. Your recipe could be chosen for one of our upcoming cookbooks!

HOME-TESTED RECIPES pil

SUBMISSION FORM
Please attach to your recipe

Name:_____

Address:_____

City:_____ **State:**____ **Zip:**_____

Phone:_____ **Email:**_____

Recipe Name:_____

Category (Check One): ❏ **Slow Cooker**   ❏ **Desserts**
                          ❏ **Casseroles**   ❏ **Cookies**

Mail to: Home-Tested Recipes, Cookbook Dept., Publications International, Ltd., 7373 N. Cicero Ave., Lincolnwood, IL 60712

Do you have your own favorite original recipe? We'd love to hear about it! Send it in, along with the submission form below. Your recipe could be chosen for one of our upcoming cookbooks!

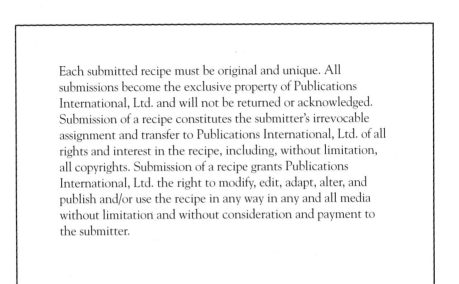

HOME-TESTED RECIPES pil

SUBMISSION FORM
Please attach to your recipe

Name:_____

Address:_____

City:_____ **State:**____ **Zip:**_____

Phone:_____ **Email:**_____

Recipe Name:_____

Category (Check One): ❏ **Slow Cooker** ❏ **Desserts**
　　　　　　　　　　　 ❏ **Casseroles** ❏ **Cookies**

Mail to: Home-Tested Recipes, Cookbook Dept., Publications International, Ltd., 7373 N. Cicero Ave., Lincolnwood, IL 60712